D1096355

52 Invitations to Grrreat *Sex*

52 Invitations to Grrreat *Sex*

Laura Corn

Park Ave Publishers

website *address:*
www.grrreatsex.com

52 Invitations To Grrreat Sex

Published by:
Park Avenue Publishers
fax (310) 452-1323
phone (602) 829-0131
P.O. Box 1453A 14th Street, Suite 116
Santa Monica, CA 90404

Website address: grrreatsex.com

All rights reserved. No part of this book may be reproduced or transmitted in any form or by any means, electronic or mechanical without the written permission of the publisher or author, except for the inclusion of brief quotations in a review.

Copyright © 1999 by Laura Corn

Library of Congress Cataloging in Publication Data
Corn, Laura

1. Sex Instruction 2. Sex 3. Man-woman relationships.
TX-0-9629629-1-2

ISBN: 0–7394–0499–7

Book Design by Total Creative, Inc.

DISCLAIMER
PLEASE READ BEFORE PROCEEDING

This book is sold with the understanding that it is intended solely for the use of informed, consenting, and hopefully monogamous adults who want to rejuvenate, enliven and sustain a great sexual relationship. The author is not a medical doctor or therapist. She has, however, studied this subject intensely for the past 8 years and is the best selling author of five books in this genre. Almost every recipe in this book has been recommend by leading sexual therapists.

The reader is cautioned that following the suggestions and scenarios contained herein is strictly voluntary and at the readers risk and discretion. Also, this book talks about sex acts which are illegal in some states. Know your state's law about sex and break them at your own risk. The positions and products mentioned in the book are safe and satisfying for the majority of adult women and men, every individual is unique and you should not employ any position or product which is not suitable to your physical or sexual limitations.

Neither the author, publisher or distributor endorses any specific product or assumes any product liability for any product mentioned in this book. The choices and responsibility for any consequences which may result form the use of any product or following any suggestion or scenario herein belong to the reader.

The author and Park Avenue Publishers, Inc., shall have neither liability nor responsibility to any person or entity with regard to any losses or damage caused or alleged to be caused, either directly or indirectly, by the information contained in this book.

If you do not wish to be bound by the above understanding, you may return the book intact to Park Avenue Publishers, Inc. P.O. Box 1453A 14th Street Santa Monica Ca, 90404 for a full refund of the purchase price of the book.

Acknowledgements

I am deeply indebted to:

Jeff Peterson – My loving punkin. Without you there would be no Grrreat Sex, either in print or in my life. Everyone who reads these books and is inspired to turn up the heat in the bedroom should know that I am inspired by *you*. (And to every woman who's ever asked if kind, decent, caring, charming, masculine, sensitive and extremely sexy men even exist, the answer is *yes*. But this one's all-l-l-lll mine!)

Marty Bishop – My friend, partner, and idol. You're a true Renaissance Man, Marty. I know people who are great with computers, or numbers, or writing, or performing, or talking to crowds... but you're the only one I know who can do it all. It's no wonder your radio show is number one. (And congratulations on those latest ratings!) Can you believe we've written four books now? I wouldn't dream of starting another one without you. Your brilliant words and special insights make these pages sparkle.

Hey, you've got someone to thank, too, don't you? [Indeed I do! My deepest appreciation to the lovely **Dawn Gonzales**, for being such a happy and willing test subject for these seductions. The research for these books sure is fun! But the actual writing can be tough, especially as deadlines approach, and I'm not sure we could have done it without the support of **Dawn** and **Jeff**. Thanks for your patience and understanding. – **M.B.**]

The crew at Login Publishers Consortium –

Susan Shaw, who gets the books out the door and spends her days solving problems for me. **Mitch**, whose a genius in finance. Thanks for all your great advice. **David Wilk**, who has a gift for taking books and turning them into best-sellers. David, you the Man!

Bill Wright, who took a chance on me when no one else would. Bill, you launched my career, and I will always be grateful for that.

Michelle Faulkner, who long ago moved from "business associate" to "great friend." Michelle, you taught me how to navigate the tricky waters of the publishing business, and I can't thank you enough for your help. You're an amazing woman – beautiful inside and out.

Meg Gallagher – My friend, through thick and thin. Meg, you've done some wonderful things for me through the years, but the greatest is letting me be godmother to your beautiful Grace.

The staff at Total Creative, who took this book and made it into a work of art –

Scott Kelly – In a perfect world, everybody would have a boss like Scott. Funny, easy to work with, and smart! **Rod** – One of those rare combinations: a talented artist with business sense and a knack for hiring great people. Exactly the kind of guy I want designing my books! **Margaret** – Oh, Margaret, I hardly know what to say. The first time I saw your gorgeous layout, the way you made my words look so beautiful, I got tears in my eyes. Marty and I relished every one of your Fed-Ex shipments, carefully displaying your finished pages around the office like the works of art they are. We were both inspired by your visual feast. **Ward** – The King of Production! Thanks for staying on top of everything. And thanks for the kind words. **Bart** – who was in charge of catching these words as they came spilling out of our Macs. That means you were the very first person to read this book! Glad you liked it.

Sharon House – The Goddess of Public Relations. I will never forget that interview with Barbara Walters on The View, and I have you to thank for it. Now when are *you* going to write a fun sex book?? You've got what it takes, honey!

Frank Weiman – Frank, I have never been more flattered. You keep bringing me offers like that, and I just know we'll do business together. Thanks for your encouragement. Don't stop calling!

Tom Davidson & William Paul at Wolfer Printing – Sealed pages, perforations, inserted invitations: this is one complicated printing project! Thanks to both of you for making it come to life.

Don & Mike – Radio gods, who are on the air in a zillion markets now. They dared me to mention them on the Barbara Walters show but, gosh, guys, it somehow... uhh, got cut out. Yes, that's right, I *raved* about you to all of America, but it ended up on the editing room floor. I made the studio audience get up and chant your names! Barbara herself did the Don & Mike Dance with me – but sadly, it never made it on the air. I'm sorry for my screw up. I really miss you guys.

Morning Mouth, Bit Board, Don Anthony & Allison, Radio Star, and all the great radio prep services who have been telling their subscribers to have me on their shows. No amount of advertising can replace a good recommendation from a respected source. Thank you.

Acknowledgements

The men and women in radio – The brightest, funniest, hardest-working people on Earth. Nearly everyone listens to the radio, so these talented deejays and programmers have a real instinct for what people want to hear. I'm delighted that they put me on, shared their audiences with me, and helped make my first three books into huge hits. Let's do it again! They are:

Jeff 'n Jer and Tommy, Kidd Kraddick, Brother Wease, Cindy & Charlie, Mancow, Johnathon Brandmeier, Buz, Carol Harmon, Tim & Mark & Mike, Mark & Brian & Frank Murphy, Don & Mike & Rob, Jim & Scott & Bob & Chris & Pepper, Connie Powell, Scott & Todd & Naomi, Lamont & Tonelli, Bob & Tom & Dean, Ron & Ron & Denise, Steve & D.C. & Courtney, Eddie Fingers, Bob Berri & Jimmy the Weasel, Jeff, Mark, & Cat, Charlie & Ty, Shelly, Dana, Kim Petersen, & Mike Rose, Troy & Rocky & Danger Boy, Kent & Allen & Leonard & Renee, Jennifer, Mike & Tyler, Chris & Beth & Kevin, Bobby & Footy, Peter Tilden & Tracy, Matt & Dave & Kathy & Merlin, Lewis & Floorwax, Rob Johnson, Lex & Teri, Dave Ryan & Pat Ebert, Kent & Allen, Paul Barsky, Grego & Moe, Donna, Brother Jake, Jeff Chambers, Jeff & Flash, Manson & Sheehan, Kevin Baker, Sheri & Bob, Tommy & Rumble, Nicki Reed, Future Bob, Opie and Anthony, G.C. Young, Max & Tanna, Moffit, Scott & Erica, Jason, Lanigan, Webster & Malone, Bob Rivers, Spike, & Downtown Joe, Rick & Leah, J.D. B.J. & Jeff, Mike & John, Eric Seidell, Johnny and Corey, Jerry Williams, Steve, Bill & The Coach, Christopher & Kerrigan, Joe & Stan, McGee & Beck, The Freakin Brothers, Kerry & Bill, T.J. & Jer, Mark Shannon & Ron Spensor, Dirk & Tom, Darla, Rick & Scott, Andy & Scott, John Patrick & Cat Thomas, Chris & Steve, Don Kelly, Allen & Karen, Pete & Dave, Mike Pentek, Eddie & Jobo, Robin & Bob, Lee Rogers, Stevens & Pruett, Brian Shannon, Danny and Rhonda Douglas, Carol Arnold, Paul & Phil, Fred, John & Richard, Gary & Erin, Susie, Dom Testa, Coach & T.K. Skywalker, Gary Burbank & Mike McConnel, Joe Elliott, Dave Otto, Dave Sposito & Ken, Mike Thomas & Steve Rouse, Samantha & Hollywood Hamilton, Jim Murphy, Tyler, Guy & Julie, Marc Anthony, Bo & Bamma, John McCormick, Tim Spencer, Bev Hart, Dan Weber, Terri Evans, Pat McMurry, John & Scott, Bucky Barker, Coffy & the Jammer, Matty in the Morning, Andy Barber, Pete McMurry, Barry Beck, Rick Moffit, Dr. Drex, Terry DiMonte, Jack Diamond & Burt, Jim Kerr, Skip & Ben, Bob Boz Bell, Jeff Walker, Willie Rich, Ben Baldwin, Larry & Willie, Paul & Phil, Greg and Bill, Susie Waud & Mark The Shark, Spike & Byron, John Lyle & Steve Hahn, Chris & Fred, Jeff Styles, Dave & The Fatman, Chris & Woody, Bob and Steve, Those Guys In The Morning, Joe Nugent, Kevin & Pete, M.C. Mitch & Rob, Ted & Marla, Phil Tower, Ted & Tom, Gina Miles, Daniels & Webster, Bax & O'Brien, Rex & Tim Parker, John & Dan & Clide, Kerry & Bill, Tommy Tucker, Ben Smith, Max Stewert, Phil & Brent, Keith & the Bearman, Billy, Super Dave & Jack, Jeff & Phil, Sam Giles, Rob Reinhart, Fanny Koeffer, Dana, Rick & Suds, Beth & Bill, Ross, Pete DeGraff, Franky C. Howie & Fizz, Jeff Slater, Ross Brittan, Dave Kirby, Dave Abbott, Lee Fowler, Buck & Peg, Greg Holt & Muddman, Mike Miller, Doug & Mike, Rick Tower, Myrna Lamb, Gary Thompson, Picozzi & The Horn, Ed, Lisa & Dr. Drai, Art Sears, Rick Moffat & Ben & Jim & Baxter, MoJo & Buckethead, Big Dave, Bill Carroll & Mike Cartalano, Chris & Rebecca, The Duke & Beth, Jerry Hart, Byrd, Mark & Lopez, Bruce Bond, John Swanson & Kathy Hart, T.C. & Dave, Much Music - Bill Welychka & Natalie Richard, Carolyn Von Vlaardingen, Art Sears, Carol & Paul Mott, Cindi Henderson, Frank Foley, Larry Norton, Darien Mckee & Colleen, Danny & the Barber, Gary Stone, Nancy Shock, Marc Razz, Ethan Carey, Larry & Lou, Steve Hansel, Johnny Danger, Lisa Butts & Mike, Ric Walker & Brad Kopeland, Gator, Josie Vogel, Dean, Roger & Joey, Mary Marlow, Scott Taylor, Larry & Willie, Nasty Man, Clay & Janice, Dave Welsh, Steve & Johnny, Katherine John, Tony Nesbitt, Sue McGarvin, Mark Benson, Randy Miller, Kimberly, Rick Lawerence & Brad & Jim Bone, John Boy & Billy, Tim & Darren, Stew Williams, Joe Mattison, Jennifer Sexton, Kevin & The Blade, Phil & Billy, Steve Ryan, Bob & Madison, Kato & Tom, Tim & Darreen, Mel & Frank, Billy Kidd & Phil, Larry & Lou, Billy & Jack, Paul Turner, Dirk Rowley, Bill & Norman, Ben Davis, Mike Spears, Steve Downs, Susan & Scott, Chris & Rebecca, Simon Will, and Thanks Again!

Table of Contents

Quickstart Guide

Sit down and read the Introduction with your lover as soon as you can. But if you want to dive right in, here's what you need to know:

1. Decide who goes first. One week you will surprise your lover with a wonderful invitation and seduction; the next week your mate will do the same for you.

2. Pick one seduction and – carefully! – tear it along the perforations down the spine. Women's pages are inscribed "For Her Eyes Only;" men's say "For His Eyes Only" (No peeking at the seductions meant for your lover's eyes).

3. Remove the enclosed invitation; read it all in private. Don't let your mate find it!

4. Fill in the blanks on the invitation. Write down the appropriate time and place, then mail it to your lover. Feel free to personalize it even more with a P.S. or a love note.

5. Gather all the necessary items: candles, lingerie, gifts, music, etc. The list of ingredients is at the bottom of each seduction. Some ingredients may be purchased at your favorite adult boutique, but if you can't find them there, call Good Vibrations™ at 1-800-289-8423.

6. On alternate weeks, when you receive an invitation, R.S.V.P. as soon as possible.

7. When the magic moment arrives and you show up for your date, throw your inhibitions out the door. Be bold!

8. A note on hygiene. Fresh breath, clean teeth, shampooed hair, and scrubbed skin – it's the uniform you put on *before* the game of love.

9. Finally – Leave this book on the nightstand or dresser in your bedroom as a constant reminder of the *grrreat* sex that awaits!

Icons printed on the first page of each seduction help you decide which one to select:

No dollar signs means it's free, or under ten dollars.	
$	10 to 25 dollars
$$	30 to 60 dollars
$$$	65 to 100 dollars
(gold star)	over 100 dollars
Car	you're going somewhere
Fork & Spoon	food is involved
Sun	you need good weather

There are lots of ways to economize, especially in the more expensive seductions. Prepare a meal at home instead of going to a fancy restaurant; dress up your bedroom rather than rent a hotel suite. Still, one or twice a year, it's important to pull out all the stops, even if you have to save up for it. Prove that your lover is worth a little sacrifice!

Just do it. *Do it do it do it!* Don't let more than two weeks slide by without tearing a page from the book. At that rate, you can look forward to two whole years of rip-roaring, sheet-splitting, mattress-melting *fun!*

SPECIAL DELIVERY

One day next week you're going to go to the mailbox. Inside will be the usual assortment of bills and ads; things to file and things to toss. But one envelope will be quite different. It'll be personalized; hand-addressed to you. You'll pull it out first, of course, and smile as you tear it open. And then your heart will skip a beat.

It's an invitation.

An invitation to have sex.

Wheee! What fun! Right there in your hand is the promise of erotic excitement, and the proof that your lover thinks you're *hot*. The invitation doesn't provide a lot of details – in fact, it could be downright mysterious, filled with clues and hints and requests for unusual objects or outfits – but there's no mistaking its purpose. On one special day, at a specific time and place, your every intimate need will be catered to. No matter how tough the week you might be facing, you know you've got a reward on the way.

And you're going to be counting the minutes until it happens!

NOT EXACTLY A SEQUEL

Four years ago I finished *101 Nights Of Grrreat Sex,* and it wasn't long before people started asking the most satisfying and terrifying question any author can hear: *Laura, when are you going to write a sequel?*

I was deeply gratified that readers loved the book so much. But more? They wanted more?! That's a tall order. I poured my heart and soul into *Grrreat Sex;* I couldn't possibly bring myself to publish anything that wasn't up to the same standard. And the whole Laura Corn message is about avoiding ruts and breaking out of routines. I didn't want to ignore my own advice and write something that was exactly the same as before.

Ah, but what if I could come up with a fun new twist to the scintillating seductions that have made the previous books such hits? Something sexy and surprising, something that adds to the burning sense of anticipation that makes each intimate encounter so exciting?

It took a while, but I did it. And I collected fifty-two brand-new seductions, some of which are hotter than ever. So even if you already have *101 Nights Of Grrreat Sex, 101 Nights Of Grrreat Romance,* or *101 Grrreat Quickies,* hold on to your hats. This book is going to take you places you've never been before... and each voyage into intimacy starts with an invitation that comes in the mail.

THE MAGIC FORMULA

Readers of my other books will recognize the invitation as an extension of my Magic Formula: *Anticipation plus Variety equals Grrreat Sex.* That's the sure cure for boredom in the bedroom, and it's built into every single seduction in this book. First, there's the excitement of waiting for the mail. Once the invitation arrives, your feeling of anticipation really starts to grow. *You have no idea what your mate is planning!* There are fifty-two surprises waiting for you; fifty-two different ways to bring each other to the heights of ecstasy.

And I don't care how long you've been together or how sexually sophisticated you might be. I guarantee there are things in here you've never tried before.

SO WHAT'S REALLY INSIDE THESE PAGES?
FIRST, THE INVITATION

Each invitation is a beautifully printed and rather steamy request for your lover to join you for some intimate fun. "Steamy" may be an understatement; some of them are downright *hot!* If the language or the suggestions are too strong for your taste, feel free to borrow my ideas and write out your own invitations. In fact, there are several that require you to customize them by filling in some blank lines. Most of them can be mailed as is, though, right after you write down the time and location of your rendezvous.

Your mate will never know quite what to expect, because no two are alike. Some are funny, some mysterious; there are riddles and rhymes and questions and promises, and a few that come with gifts attached. Every single one is a big fat tease, designed to keep your lover bouncing with excitement as your erotic adventure draws closer.

SECOND, THE SEDUCTION

Each page tells you exactly what to do in order to pull off a thrilling sexual seduction. Many of them require props: sometimes simple items you might have around the house or can get at any department store, and sometimes toys that can be purchased at adult stores. (The sex toys can also be ordered through the Good Vibrations™ catalog if you can't find them at your favorite local adult boutique; see the Quickstart Guide.) Improvise! Customize, if you wish. But you'll have a perfectly *grrreat* time if you do nothing but follow the recipe exactly as written.

Some of these seductions will certainly challenge you to be bolder than you've ever been in your life. You might read one of these and say to yourself, "Laura Corn, I just can't do that!" To which I say:

Yes, you can. Hundreds of thousands of couples have already taken the plunge ahead of you. And over the years I've heard from hundreds of women who say the same thing: they were a little nervous at first... *but the book gave them permission to do it.*

I just love that phrase. They had *permission* to do it, to be wicked and aggressive, to be highly sexual and naughty, to wear hot outfits and perform new acts of pleasure, because they were following the instructions in the book.

So go ahead. Surprise your mate. Shock your lover. I said it's okay.

LAURA, WE HAVE *KIDS!*

My short answer:

Where there's a will, there's a way. Or to be more precise, where there's a couple of highly aroused grownups, there's a way!

Here's the longer answer. Most of the couples who buy my books have kids, and they've come up with some creative solutions. The basic rule is that if it's your week to seduce, it's your responsibility to do something with the children. Babysitters? Relatives? Neighbors? Whatever you might do to have an evening out, you should do in order to have a private evening *in*. (Although there are a lot of seductions here that take you out of the bedroom... and out of the house!)

Whatever you do with the children, though, please don't hide your excitement from them. Let them see how thrilled you are to be spending some intimate time with your mate. Expose them to the flirting and laughing and hugging that goes along with a healthy marriage. You're their role models, after all; don't you want them to learn to be as happy and affectionate and well-adjusted as you?

HOW TO DO IT

You *don't* go through the seductions from front to back, all in a row. That's too predictable; you won't want your lover to know what's coming. (And no peeking to see what pages your sweetheart has selected!) When it's your turn to be the seducer, pick up the book and leaf through it. Check out the icons on each title page; they give you a clue about what to expect. The little dollar signs indicate the amount of money you might have to spend to pull off your adventure, which will help you budget your romance dollars; if you're a bit too close to payday, for instance, pick one that's free. A few of the seductions are pretty expensive, and I suggest you save those for special occasions like birthdays, anniversaries, and Valentine's Day. But most of these cost less than twenty dollars, and it's easy to find ways to economize. The meaning of all the icons is spelled out on the Quickstart Page.

Once you decide on a seduction, carefully tear it from the book along the spine, and look it over. Find the invitation and fill in the blanks, put it in an envelope, and mail it to your lover. Then gather up the necessary ingredients (they're listed at the bottom of each seduction), follow the instructions, and get ready for a day, a night, or even a weekend of *grrreat* sex!

So who goes first? Well, that's up to you. Read this introduction together and talk it over. But once you start, leave the book on your nightstand, right next to your bed. As soon as your lover has sprung a fabulous, exciting and extremely satisfying seduction on you, it's your turn to pick up the book and tear out a page.

You don't have to do it every week, but I urge you not to let much time pass between seductions; no more than two weeks. (At that rate, by the way, this book will give you *two full years* of thrilling new sexual experiences. What a bargain!) If you walk into the bedroom and the book has moved from the nightstand to your pillow, well, I'd take that as a hint that you've fallen behind. Pick it up and get busy.

A lot of couples enjoy scheduling a regular date to sit down together and read through the titles before tearing out a page. Sunday night seems to be the favorite, after the kids are in bed and the house is quiet. But there are no hard-and-fast rules, other than these:

1: *Alternate*. You seduce your mate, then your mate seduces you. And 2: *Do it!*

WHAT CAN YOU EXPECT?

More sex, of course. Better sex! And within weeks, you'll discover – or *re*-discover – a broader and deeper level of intimacy. The power of these invitations stems from two things that are critical to a healthy relationship: *anticipation* and *commitment*.

First, your lover will get a thrill when your special delivery arrives. It's the same rush you both felt when you first started dating, and that sense of anticipation is only going to grow through the week. The thought that your mate has been working for *days* to plan an intimate encounter is enough to put a smile – and a blush! – on anyone's face.

Second, there's no way *not* to follow through with your promise. You can't put it off; once that envelope drops in the mail chute, there's no turning back! For many couples, this will be the first time in years that sex will be given as much priority as everything else. You schedule time for work, and bills, and family... and now intimacy will find a permanent spot on your calender.

Before you know it, great sex will be a habit!

SO GET STARTED, ALREADY. TEAR THIS BOOK APART!

Over a million couples have now followed my recipes for seduction. Thousands of them have written and called to tell me about their own special erotic tricks and bedroom treats, and many of those stories formed the foundations of this book. If you recognize yourself in here – thank you. I couldn't have written it without you.

And thank *you* for buying this book! Your reward is waiting inside, so go ahead, start right now. Tear out a page, read the seduction, fill out the invitation and slip it into an attractive envelope. The moment you drop it in the mail, the clock starts ticking....

Wishing you a lifetime of love and *grrreat* sex,

Laura Corn
Santa Monica, California
January 1999

52 Invitations to Grrreat *Sex*

52 Invitations to Grrreat Sex

n u m b e r **I**

Stand Back! I Don't Know How Big
This Thing Is Going to Get!

For Her Eyes Only

"An erection is a mysterious thing. There's always that fear, each time one goes, that you won't be seeing it again."

-Kirk Douglas

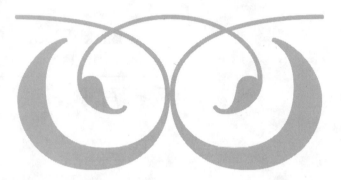

n u m b e r **I**

Stand Back! I Don't Know How Big This Thing Is Going to Get!

i n g r e d i e n t s

• 1 cup of hot tea, or any warm drink you like   • 1 warm and very busy mouth
• 1 glass of ice cubes, melting

He Brings
1 necktie (for blindfold)
1 serving tray
2 snowballs

As I write this, my previous book, *101 Nights Of Grrreat Sex*, has sold well over half a million copies. That's a lot of happy customers! I get plenty of feedback from them, and the seduction that always generates the most praise is Number 5, "The Velvet Tongue." It's based on a simple trick used by call girls to put men completely over the top, and frankly, I never thought it could be beat. And then I remembered what my high school boyfriend used to say after an evening of serious smooching:

"Oh, wow; I gotta take a cold shower...."

Ever hear a guy say that after he gets all hot and bothered, but isn't allowed to finish? Not recently, I hope! It happens to all boys when they're young and single, and even to grown men when something interrupts foreplay – and when it does, you just have to feel sorry for them. They're stuck with this **big throbbing thing** between their legs that simply doesn't understand the word, "no!" That's when a blast of icy water is called for. It's basic science: everything, including those little love machines, *contracts* when it gets cold. (You might have seen a Seinfeld episode that was devoted to the rather embarrassing problem of "shrinkage!")

That's what gave me the idea for the greatest sexual technique I have ever discovered. And you are about to learn it.

Your invitation is quite mysterious this week. You're asking your lover to bring a tie and a *tray* to the bedroom. Set them aside at first; you won't need them for the long kisses and mutual **striptease** that begin your evening. But once you're both warmed up, ask him to turn around while you blindfold him with the necktie. Sure, men are visual creatures; they like to *see* you having sex. But this time, you don't want anything to distract from the rather intense physical sensations you have in store... and you don't want him to know when they're coming!

Have him lay on his back, and place the tray on the bed next to him. Go to the kitchen for your secret ingredients: *hot* and *cold*. That is, a mug of tea or some other hot liquid, and ice cubes swimming in a glass of water. Put them on the tray. Now play with his penis... and his mind.

Squeeze his shaft; draw it into your mouth. Tease it the way you might on any other night. Then invoke the magic of The Velvet Tongue. Take a sip of hot tea and let the warmth flood your mouth. Don't swallow it all; try to hold a bit of steamy liquid as you plunge your lips past the head of his trembling erection. *Ohhhh...* a sigh escapes from your lover as the unexpected warmth envelopes his most tender part. Like flame under a kettle, the few minutes of added heat brings him to a simmer, but before he can boil over...

... pop a half-melted ice cube in your mouth and dive back down the length of his shaft. His entire body will twitch with the shock; he'll gasp as his buttocks rise off the bed. Just a few seconds is all you need, and probably all he can take, before you switch back to your overheated mouth. This battle can go on for quite a long while. The warmth draws blood to the surface, swelling his already engorged rod; the chill keeps him from coming too fast. The control, needless to say, is all yours. The pressure will build through several cycles of this **exquisite** torture until he's ready to pump gallons.

This, of course, is the exact opposite of the condition for which those boys needed a cold shower. They used to call it "blue balls," remember? Well, I have a name for this kind of explosive super-orgasm:

Snowballs. Frosty had 'em, too. Which explains why he was such a jolly, happy soul!

"An erection is a mysterious thing.
There's always that fear, each
time one goes, that you won't be
seeing it again."

-Kirk Douglas

Sex is merely Sex

Until you experience the hottest trick
in the book

It requires **One Necktie**, *color irrelevant*,

One Serving Tray, *empty,*

and **One extremely aroused Partner,**

willing to demonstrate something New and slightly Nasty in the bedroom

You bring the first two. The third will be waiting to

blow you away

Location:_____

Date:_____

Time:_____

R.S.V.P. Lift my knees over your shoulders.

Slide your face between my thighs. One lick means "no".

Two licks means "yes"

(500 licks means "ohhhmigawd-yes-yes-yes-please-don't-stop-oh-YESSSS!")

52 Invitations to Grrreat Sex

n u m b e r **2**

She's Out of Control $

For His Eyes Only

"All too many men still seem to believe, in a rather naive and egocentric way, that what feels good to them is automatically what feels good to women."

-Shere Hite, sex researcher and best selling author

n u m b e r **2**

She's Out of Control

i n g r e d i e n t s

- Several candles
- Hot music
- One long silk scarf
- Two short lengths of nylon rope (I got mine at Target. Check it before you buy, though – you want the smooth, soft kind that feels almost like velvet.)

- One vibrator (Good for you if she has one! But if you want to surprise her, consider buying a new Pocket Rocket™ – you'll also need it for another seduction. And if you've got a fatter budget, try the world's best-seller, the venerable Magic Wand™, by Hitachi.)

She Brings:
One large pillow
One wooden hanger
And the time to hang around

Equal Schmequal. Tonight, *you* will be the **Master**; she will be your **servant**. And she will learn the intensely erotic pleasures of sexual submission.

Your roles must be established as soon as she meets you at the bedroom door. As Commander, you are charming and pleasant, but give no more information than she needs. Why did she bring the large pillow, as spelled out in your invitation? Why the sturdy wooden coat hanger? *"Oh, you'll see,"* you say, slyly and smoothly. *"Or, actually, you won't see. I don't want to spoil the surprise."*

At this point you pass a long silk scarf across her eyes, and tie it behind her head. Ask her to hold the hanger, gripping the ends, then – while telling her how lovely she is, and how much you've been thinking of her – *tie her wrists to the hanger.*

Gently press her back to the bedroom door. Lift her arms over her head, and then hook the hanger over the top of the door. **Caress** her; kiss her neck. *"Wha... what are you doing?"* she'll no doubt ask. *"Why... whatever I want to, I guess. And, oh my goodness, there doesn't seem to be anything you can do about it, does there?"* Squeeze her nipple, kiss her face. Tell her to be a good girl, do exactly what her Master says, and she'll get a great **big surprise**. *"I have a few things to do... and I want you to stay right here, where I can... mmm, well... play with you."*

Go start the stereo, light some candles, arrange some pillows. But every time you finish a task, walk up to her and touch her, caress her, kiss her. Unzip this, unbutton that. Lead her, bound and blindfolded, through the slowest and most sensuous strip tease of her life. This time, though, it's *you* who is doing the teasing.

Finally, it's time to free her hands and bring her to your special Altar of Eros: a pile of pillows – including the one she brought, of course – laid on the floor at the foot of the bed. Resting at its center: electric magic. Possibly the greatest invention of the century. A vibrator, charged and ready for action.

Instruct her to **kneel**, facing the bed and straddling the pillows, and adjust the toy so that it is in *just* the right place. Sit on the edge of the bed directly in front of her; let her watch, wide-eyed and aroused, as you slowly squeeze and stroke your swelling **manhood**. *"And now, my little slave, you have a very important job to do. It will demand your total concentration and focus. You must take this"* – the stiffening erection now rubbing against her face, sliding across her lips – *"and make it feel just as good... as that...."*

Turn on **the vibrator**. Set the remote control to slow, at first; it will be more than enough to make her quiver. *"Let's see what a good little servant you can be. Let's see how much you want to please your Master."*

Vary the speed. Slowly notch it up, accelerating the cycle of **arousal**. Chase that delicious buzz from her lips to your erection to the controller to the toy to her pulsing little clit and straight up her electrified spine, around and around until she explodes, her muffled scream barely escaping her full mouth, back arching, **thighs trembling**, eyes clenched tight against the brilliant orgasmic light flooding her body, your own juices flooding her eager mouth.

I have a prediction to make. The next time she's with her girlfriends and they start to complain about the way their men monopolize the remote control, I bet your sweetheart will simply smile, and blush. *"Maybe,"* she'll say, *"They just don't know how to use it right...."*

"All too many men still seem to believe, in a rather naive and egocentric way, that what feels good to them is automatically what feels good to women."

-Shere Hite, sex researcher and best selling author

The Depths Of A Secret
And Deeply Erotic Fantasy

will be explored this

———————————— evening at ———— p.m.

In preparation for this sensuous journey towards an entirely

new peak of sexual arousal, you are required to present:

One Large Pillow and

One Wooden Hanger

at the boudoir entrance.

R.S.V.P.

(Be Prepared to Lose Control)

52 Invitations to Grrreat Sex

n u m b e r 3

Kinky Kisses

For Her Eyes Only

It's the good girls who keep the diaries; the bad girls never have the time.

-Tallulah Bankhead

number 3

Kinky Kisses

i n g r e d i e n t s

- 1 Car (with back seat!)
- 1 Garage (or secluded, safe spot)
- 1 scarf (for blindfold)
- Soft nylon rope (or – *ooh!* – silky stockings!)

- Music (sexy and loud)
- Perfume (brand new)
- And for extra credit: a wig (He'll be wigged out when he feels someone *else's* hair)

He Brings
Sunglasses
A trouserful of anticipation

"What were you _thinking??!!!_"

Like everyone watching that night, I howled with laughter when Jay Leno asked that question of Hugh Grant. Remember him? He's the extremely embarrassed British actor who made headlines all over the world following his arrest for soliciting a prostitute. What _was_ he thinking?! Hugh is famous, rich and engaged to **gorgeous supermodel** Elizabeth Hurley, and he risked all that for a hummer from the improbably-named Divine Brown.

I'll tell you what he was thinking: _I'm about to get a blowjob in a car!_ Yep, that's all. That's all he _could_ think, I imagine. Such is the incredible power of the connection between sex and automobiles. It's a bond that gets forged early. Most of us have our first erotic experiences in a car, and for men especially, that link becomes a driving force, pardon the pun, through their entire lives. Hey, who do you think is buying those gigantic four-wheel-drive Suburban Assault Vehicles you see all over the roads these days? America doesn't have _that_ many **lumberjacks**. Does anyone else think it's funny that the biggest and meanest car you can legally drive is actually called a Hummer??

Because of that connection, sex is used to sell cars – just check out any automobile ad – and sex is better _in_ cars. It's a lesson your lover is going to learn all over again this week.

It starts when he meets you for your date, wondering why you asked him to bring sunglasses in the evening. _"You'll see,"_ you can say as you lead him to the garage. _"Or rather, you won't see. Come here."_ Pull out a scarf and **blindfold** your sweetie, then put the shades on his face. _"Now lean forward against the car... and put your hands behind your back."_ Pull out a second scarf and tie his wrists together, then guide him onto the back seat. Fire up the engine, and crank up the music. _"You just sit there and be a good boy. We're going for a little ride...."_

Where to? That depends on where you live, of course. A quiet side street? An isolated parking lot? Safety and privacy are your two biggest concerns, and so here's my best suggestion: drive around enough to confuse your mate, and then _pull into your own garage._ Or maybe borrow one from an understanding friend. The point is that he shouldn't know where he is... and he really won't know what's going on when you get out of the car. _"Stay right here. I'll be back in a while."_

Two minutes later, the back door opens. Someone **crawls** in. He thinks it's you, but he gets no answer to his questions. There's a lovely new fragrance in the air, one he's never smelled before. But he's pretty sure it's you. It _is_ you, isn't it...?

It doesn't matter anymore. He's swept away by the sheer eroticism of the moment. Hands pull at his zipper. Fingers wrap around his rapidly-swelling cock and pull it free, **squeezing and stroking** and rubbing it until it's a pillar of stone. Suddenly, soft lips caress the tip, then slide down the shaft, engulfing his entire penis. He feels the suction, the friction, the excitation as an eager head bounces up and down in his lap. He's bound, and blind, and not sure where he is; his entire universe consists only of his raging erection and the hungry mouth around it.

It is, as the very proper Mr. Grant might say, a Divine experience!

It's the good girls who keep the diaries; the bad girls never have the time.

-Tallulah Bankhead

Do You Like Riddles?

I have a plan to drive you Mad with Passion and if you are

victorious in Exposing my Secret, I will grant you any wish.

It's on the tip of your fingers—or rather, your Four fingers and a Thumb.

Not coming to you? Then I shall Simply Surprise you with my

Erotic and Decadent

Kinky Kisses

The mystery unfolds this_____

starting at_____o'clock.

Meet me:_____

And Wear Your Sunglasses

R.S.V.P. with a Kinky Kiss of your own, planted anywhere

that I do NOT have a tan

52 Invitations to Grrreat Sex

n u m b e r 4

Get Crazy $

For Her Eyes Only

They made love as though they were an endangered species.

-Peter de Vries

number 4

Get Crazy

*T*reasure this document. It contains the accumulated sexual experience of thousands of happy men.

When my *101 Nights of Grrreat Sex* first came out, I began keeping track of the calls I got from satisfied customers. Several hundred radio shows later, I can tell you exactly what fantasies and techniques American guys love the most.

And right here on this page I have combined the top four favorites into one long, fabulous, outrageous, over-the-top, guaranteed-to-please seduction. It's the ultimate fantasy for any man: seventy-two hours of pleasure, all initiated by his lover, with no chance of failure or rejection.

Welcome to the Great Sex Weekend.

Friday night you are the **Sultry Seductress**. This one may actually be more fun for *you* than for him, and it's certainly simple. All you have to do is look great and act interested; he'll take care of the rest. Flirtatious kisses and caresses lead to a slow striptease. You shimmy out of your skirt, you slither out of your blouse and then – *pow!* – you smack him right in the head with an incredibly erotic image: a body stocking. It's so much more arousing than bra and panties. It's a visual contradiction – "I'm completely covered, and completely naked." He can *almost* touch you behind that sheer layer of fabric, and that last translucent millimeter makes you incredibly enticing. In a word, it's hot. No wonder men pick the body stocking as the top choice for erotic clothing. Me, I just love to wear them – and I adore the reaction I get when I do!

Saturday morning is a "quickie" – a fast chase to a powerful **orgasm**. *His* orgasm, in this case. Ideally, you will wake him up with your sweet lips wrapped around the *fastest growing erection you have ever seen in your life*. I've never found a man who could find words to describe the awesome sensation of coming to consciousness with a wet, wild, enthusiastic blowjob. It is, as one caller put it, a spiritual experience. If he's already awake, then snag him before he gets out of bed, and be sure to make it clear that this treat is strictly for him. You'll get your reward another time, but right now it's suck, shower, and face the day with a smile!

The single most popular seduction in my *101 Nights Of Grrreat Romance* is called "Sleepless In The Saddle," and it takes place early Sunday morning. Very early. *Three o'clock in the morning.* Set your internal alarm, and as soon as it goes off, get up and light a single candle. As with yesterday's quickie, your goal is to wake him with sex, but this time you get in on the action, too. Use your hands and mouth to rouse him, and when he's **good and hard**, straddle him and slip his shaft inside. Make love slowly, gently and silently, as if in a dream state. Blow out the candle when it's over, and sink back into the pillows for the deepest, most satisfying sleep possible.

By Sunday afternoon, your mate's libido will be turbocharged. There's nothing that makes you eager for more sex like, well, lots of sex! And today you're going to pull out all the stops. Prepare a smorgasbord of sensual treats: parade in your panties. Eat snacks in the sack. Massage his back; take a shower á deux. Rent a really sexy movie, or even an adult video, and keep your fingers wrapped around his balls throughout. Pose for him in the naughtiest positions you can imagine, and when at last he plunges his throbbing erection into you, **moan and gasp** and whimper and beg as if his every touch propels you into a higher orgasmic orbit. Courtesan, geisha, hooker, cheerleader; you're everything he's ever dreamed of.

Well, okay, you're not a Heismann Trophy or a ninety-nine yard kickoff return. So if it's football season, I suggest you wait until after the final whistle to start your seduction. You know how men are with their games.

Fortunately, they haven't figured out that only *we* know the score!

They made love as though they were an endangered species.

-Peter de Vries

Welcome To The
Great Sex Weekend

You are going to be jumped and stroked and kissed and fondled and teased

and stripped and bathed and licked and nibbled and swallowed and totally,

thoroughly, completely

F**ked

The clock is ticking...

...and the only advice I can offer is:

Don't work late This Friday

(In fact, you would be well advised to cancel all appointments this weekend.

You do not want to miss this boat.)

The favor of a reply is requested.

You can write your answer on a card and mail it to me.

Or you can chase me through the house,

toss me on the bed, and give it to me orally.

52 Invitations to Grrreat Sex

n u m b e r 5

Body Blast $

For His Eyes Only

"Sex is one of the nine reasons for reincarnation.
The other eight are unimportant."

-Henry Miller

n u m b e r **5**

Body Blast

i n g r e d i e n t s

- 1 ice pack (preferably self-chilling, like the Super-Cool™ Cold Pack)

- 2 instant warmers (I recommend Sports Heat® Hand Warmers. Note: Don't get them wet. Before the seduction, put a single layer of Saran Wrap around one to use on her moist parts.)

She Brings:
1 blindfold
1 very promising forecast

Skin.

It's just amazing, isn't it? It can be tough as a sailor's hands, or smooth as a baby's bottom. The same stuff that can be banged and scraped without permanent damage can also sense the gentlest draft, the lightest touch. When we talk about **erogenous zones**, we're really talking about skin, and the way it translates pressure into erotic sensations. Cybersex will never replace the real thing until some genius figures out how to get skin involved.

And yet we often miss its full potential. Hey, kissing's great, and nothing beats a slow nibble in the right spot! But the skin can can get aroused by more than friction. Like the brain itself, skin gets most turned on when pushed to extremes.

Now, if you're thinking whips and nipple clamps, pal, you've got the wrong book. (Or at least the wrong chapter! You never know what surprises your lover and I have worked up for you.) No, this week's seduction concentrates on extremes of temperature, and to pull it off you need to buy *hand warmers* and ***cold packs***.

There are some cold packs that have to sit in your freezer, but my favorite is the one that chills the instant you squish it and mix some internal chemicals. You can find them in any drug store. You might have to go to a ski shop to get hand warmers; skiers tuck them inside gloves and socks.

Of course, your mate is going to be plenty hot to start with – she's been burning with curiosity since she opened the mail, because your invitation asked her to bring a blindfold. Don't give anything away when she greets you at the door, though. **Kiss her**; share a glass of wine. And then... *"Are you ready?"* For what, she's dying to know. *"Mmm, you'll see. Oh, gosh, I guess you won't see, will you? Poor baby.... You'll just have to wait to find out...."*

Tie the scarf over her eyes and lead her to the bedroom. Take your time and enjoy the view while you undress her. Ask her to lay on her tummy, then start your special massage by rubbing her feet. After a few minutes, surprise her with a heated warmer. You'll hear a moan as the incredible sensation **spreads** through one foot – and a sharp squeal when an ice pack touches the other. Switch back and forth as you work your way up. The backs of her knees, the tops of her thighs, the base of her neck – always a short shot of cold followed by a minute of deep, sensual warmth.

With the blindfold on, she can never know just which sensation is going to strike next, or precisely where. But the reaction will be the same down the front of her body: a gasp of shock, a deep sigh of relaxation. Focus on her breasts and her **nipples**, and all those tense muscles that connect at the hip. Break out a fresh pack of warmers for the grand finale. Part her legs and caress her clitoris with a handful of glowing warmth; alternate with your buzzing tongue. At the same time slip a bag of radiant heat between the cheeks of her butt. Press it directly against her ass and the delicate perineum; trust me, this sensation is awesome, overwhelming, staggering, arousing.

Such intense extremes in such a confined area will have much the same effect as it does with the weather. Cold fronts slam into hot zones, generating wild winds of pleasure and crackling bolts of **erotic electricity**. With a lot of skill and a little luck, you just might find yourself swept away by the ultimate in orgasmic storms: *the sexual tornado*.

Nothing on earth sucks as well.

*"Sex Is One Of The Nine
Reasons For Reincarnation. The
Other Eight Are Unimportant."*

-Henry Miller

Batten Down The Hatches

A Sexual Storm

is about to be unleashed across your body.

Your skin will be charged with erotic electricity; you will

get quite wet.

You will need no umbrella, no raincoat.

You are asked to bring only one item:

a Blindfold.

Yes, you will be required to wear it.

No, you will not know where the wild winds lead us.

Your journey into the heart of the storm begins

_____ evening at _____ p.m.

Meet me _____ .

R.S.V.P. by leaving your favorite panties

on the front seat of my car.

52 Invitations to Grrreat Sex

n u m b e r 6

The Velvet Massage

For Her Eyes Only

I think I made his back feel better.

-Marilyn Monroe, after a private meeting with John F. Kennedy

n u m b e r **6**

The Velvet Massage

i n g r e d i e n t s

- Candles, lit
- Mirror, if possible
- Massage oil, warm

- Lover, hot
- Confidence, unleashed

He Brings:
One small bowl or goblet for the oil
One aching back
One happy front!

What do men find most appealing in a woman?

Self-confidence. It's the ultimate aphrodisiac.

Marilyn Monroe had it in spades – or at least she was able to act like it, which amounts to the same thing. Legend says she had a special bedroom trick that dazzled the minds and scorched the bodies of some mighty famous and – *wink, wink* – politically **powerful men**. I made that technique the centerpiece of a hugely popular seduction called "I Think I Made His Back Feel Better" in my *101 Nights Of Grrreat Sex*. Now over half a million couples have learned what Marilyn knew: that a woman who can take control of an intimate encounter and please herself while *pleasing her* lover can keep any man hot and bothered and begging for more.

Believe it or not, I found a way to improve it....

Your sweetheart will greet you at the bedroom door with a small, elegant bowl in his hand. Put it on the nightstand, then unbutton his shirt. Lead him to the bed and ask him to lay on his **tummy**, and if it's at all possible, make sure he can see your reflection in a mirror. Don't have one you can move around? You'll need one for another seduction anyway; go ahead and get one of those ten-dollar dressing mirrors at Target and prop it up on the wall, right in front of your lover's face.

Slowly, as if performing a sacred ritual, walk around the room lighting some candles. You're in charge tonight, and to make that point, slap his hands away if he tries to help you remove his clothing. After he's bare – and barely able to contain his growing sense of anticipation – you'll undress, letting him watch every **sensual move**.

Pour warm massage oil into the bowl, and dip your fingers into it. Rub it all over his left foot. *And then straddle it.* Press his heel against that secret, special spot. Slither your way down to his toes, spreading oil with your bushy little brush. Use his foot to please yourself. And no matter how much he wants to... don't let him help. All the erotic power in your body, perhaps the greatest power in the world, is concentrated in that pretty little puss, and you're about to use it to give him the rubdown of a lifetime – a Velvet Massage.

Inch your Velvet Clit up his leg, drizzling oil along the way. Look in the mirror; do you see the fire burning in his eyes? He'll be wild with lust as you knead his powerful calf muscles with your thighs; out of his mind by the time you slide your sex across his bare bottom. Move up a bit more. There's one special place you're aiming for, and I call it "Marilyn's Spot." It's just under the tailbone, just above your lover's **buttocks**, and after a liberal application of scented oil, you're going to nestle your aching clit right against it... and *push.*

Stretch out across your mate's back; run your fingers down to his own and grab his hands. Let him feel the weight of your breasts against his back. Let him hear you moan in his ear as you chase your own pleasure. The sight of you in the mirror, writhing against his **naked flesh**, will be seared forever into his eyes. When you're ready, start to bump and rock and wriggle and grind your way back down his other leg. Every thrust of your hips will show him how aroused you are; every gasp proves his power to turn you on. See if you can make it all the way to his foot before unleashing your climax. Your explosive, shattering orgasm will be almost enough to give him one of his own.

Almost! Once you've caught your breath, you've still got a little more work to do. No doubt you've noticed the bedsheets slowly creeping in from the edges. They're not shrinking, they're disappearing – straight down the hole he's been punching in the bed!

Gently **unplug** him from the mattress... and plug him into you.

"I think I made his back

feel better."

-Marilyn Monroe,
after a private meeting with John F. Kennedy

Sexual Secrets

Sensual moves.

Erotic Techniques.

Bedroom tricks.

Every woman has them.

And you're about to learn one of mine . . .

*Lesson begins at:*_____

*Date:*_____

*Location :*_____

Bring an apple for your teacher

in a small china bowl or goblet

(If you're good, I'll keep you after class!)

You may R.S.V.P. by post, telegram, or email.

But it would be so much more fun to do it orally!

52 Invitations to Grrreat Sex

n u m b e r 7

Touching Fire $

FOR HIS EYES ONLY

"Oh, not at all-just a straight-away pounder."

-Lily Langtry, On being asked if the Prince of Wales was a romantic lover

n u m b e r 7

Touching Fire

i n g r e d i e n t s

- Candles (Dozens! All white)
- Candle holders
- Her favorite robe
- Her favorite beverage
- More candles! (And no pets to knock them over)
- 2 notes
- 1 chair

- 1 quart milk
- Still more candles (And no children to play with them)
- Bubble bath
- Massage oil
- Pajamas (When was the last time you wore anything but an old t-shirt at night? Women adore a well-dressed man, and that goes for nightclothes, too. Think "PJ's for BJ's!")

One day in the near future your sweetheart will be sitting with her girlfriends and they'll be talking — surprise! — about men. One of them will mention how her boyfriend bought her a dozen red roses for her birthday. *Oooh,* the rest will mutter, *how nice.* Another will brag that her husband took her to see Cats, and the rest will coo and cluck and assure her that he must be very sweet indeed. A sly smile will spread across your mate's face. *"Well, let me tell you what <u>my</u> guy did...."*

Your invitation instructed her to be home precisely on time. The reason is clear as soon as she opens the door; the only illumination in the house is from candles. Lots and lots of them, mostly inexpensive little votive candles, set in holders and tin trays and saucers. The one closest to the door has a note sitting under it: *Follow the Lights.*

A-ha! It's a trail, and the next closest candle leads in the direction of the dining room. A few **flickering lights** later she's at the table, on which rests a glass of wine and another note. *Sit. Relax. Take your shoes off. Enjoy a drink. But don't be long... I'm waiting at the end of the trail....*

The lights lead across the living room to a small table with a box. The note on it says *"Undress, put this on, and come find me,"* and inside she sees her favorite robe. The stress and aggravations of the day are starting to melt away, replaced by the sensual buzz of anticipation. She follows the lights down the hall into the bedroom, and breaks into a big grin when she sees you lounging in a brand-new pair of sexy, **silky** pajamas. Her adventure hasn't ended yet, though. You point out the candles leading to the bathroom, now steamed up from the hot bath you drew as soon as you heard her come in the front door. What luxury — it's a ***milk bath***, with a quart or so of whole milk and a few capfuls of scented bubble bath mixed in. She sits and soaks and nibbles the hors d'ouvres you're serving from your tubside seat.

Now she's three quarters of the way to paradise, and you're about to escort her right through the gates. Towel her off, and take her back to the bedroom. Across the floor there's an entire constellation of candles encircling a pile of pillows and a blanket. Mmm... it's **rubdown time**. You drizzle warm massage oil onto her back, forming pretty patterns across her back. Work the oil out her arms and through her fingers, and down her legs onto her toes. Concentrate on her gleaming, buttery-soft buttocks; slide a slick, slippery finger right between the cheeks of her ass. Gently probe the folds of woman-flesh hidden between her thighs. They're hot now, and swelling as blood rushes to supply her tingling nerves.

One finger, dripping with oil, circles her clit; she gasps as you begin to stroke it. Another finger slips past her full lips and enters her, tap-tap-tapping against her G-Spot. Suddenly she feels the weight of your wood as you straddle her butt, gliding your erection up and down her lubricated cheeks. She focuses on the head of your cock as you move it down, down, between her **thighs**, pressing against her labia, past them, between them, going in. Deeper, pushing harder, until her ass is spread wide against your hips, the full weight of your body behind every thrust, a huge wet lip-biting back-arching climax growing closer with every stroke.

At this point in her story, the girlfriends will be silent, jaws dropped. One of them might manage a dry croak. *"Uh, well... you win."* The others can only nod.

You'll know when she's told her erotic tale. You'll walk into one of their gatherings, the conversation will come to a halt, and every eye will be on you.

Walk proud, man. They're envious.

"Oh, not at all-just a straight-away pounder."

-Lily Langtry, On being asked if the Prince of Wales was a romantic lover

You Are The Center
Of My World

Your devoted lover desires only to please you

and arouse you and caress you and tease you

and suck you and hold you and worship you

and Make You Come

very hard, very many times.

Your presence in requested at a ceremony honoring your

Supremely Sensual Beauty

beginning exactly at ——————— o'clock

this———————————————evening

It is essential to the success of the Festivities that you be gone

at least One Hour before the appointed time, and appear at

——————— precisely on schedule.

To signify your acceptance, please present one lovely nipple

to my waiting lips

52 Invitations to Grrreat Sex

number 8

No Escape

FOR HIS EYES ONLY

"In my sex fantasy, nobody ever loves me for my mind."

-Nora Ephron

number 8

No Escape

i n g r e d i e n t s

- Sexy music (My pick? Romanza, by Andrea Bocelli. This is a seduction of contrasts: she's aroused, yet helpless. Powerfully romantic music is almost the opposite of sexual domination. Believe me, it works. Play it loud!)
- Soft nylon rope (or a scarf)
- Adult boutique, if available

- Eros™ moisturizing lubricant (or other non-staining massage oil)
- Pocket Rocket™ (one of many tiny vibrators on the market)
- Drive-through restaurant for milk shake and straw

She Brings
Blanket
Skirt
She Does Not Bring
Panties!
Or any way to stop you...

Lovers are getting tied up all *over* the place!

Thirty to forty percent of the couples in America occasionally indulge in light bondage fantasies. Or, as Bob Berkowitz calls it, "Decaf S&M." In the book "His Secret Life," Bob writes that a lot of people have already ventured into Marquis de Sade territory without knowing it. Whips and chains?? No way! But have you ever pinned your lover's arms to the bed while making love? Uh, yeah; sure, she loves it.

And here's why she loves it: you're taking away the option to *not* enjoy **sex**. Good girls aren't supposed to, you know. But when your leather belt is wrapped around her wrists, well, the good little girl is helpless... and the naughty little slut is free at last!

Your mate will already be a bit aroused when she meets you for your big date. There's something about wearing a skirt with no panties underneath that's just so... I don't know. **Wicked**. Free. Sexual. You also asked her to bring a blanket, so she's probably assuming a picnic – *Ha!* Toss it into the back of the car, then tell her to get in the passenger seat and buckle up. Now ask her to close her eyes. Quickly toss two loops of soft, slick nylon rope over her wrists and cinch them up. Not too tight! The rope then gets tied to the seat belt so she can't move her hands. **Hike her skirt** up to her hips, exposing her sacred spot.

Get behind the wheel and start your amorous adventure. Her cheeks will flush at the thought that she's so exposed as you drive along. That rush of fear is balanced by the extraordinary sensation of your fingers **stroking her**, caressing her, diddling her while you calmly make your way through traffic. No one can tell what's going on down there... but *she* knows, the thought is at once terrifying and exhilarating.

Your first stop is the drive-through lane at a fast food joint. Uh-oh. The girl at the window will be able to see her. She tries to cover her thatch with her immobile hands. *No, no, please, don't let her, I don't want to, honey....*

At the last second you reach behind the seat, pull out the blanket, and throw it over her lap. *Whew!* Get your milk shake and head for an empty corner of a big parking lot. Expose her again, and play some more. Take your straw and drip a big glob of frosty cream right on **her love box** – then lean over and lap it up. Her brain will be spinning by now. It's still daylight, there are people and cars within sight, and she's getting head right there in the car! She couldn't stop you if she wanted to; she's completely at your mercy and literally out of control.

Next stop: an adult toy store, if your town has one. Leave her in the car, blanket over her naked flesh, doors locked. She knows she's safe and secure – and at the same time a voice is screaming *you're tied up! Your bare butt is on the car seat!!* Once inside, buy some **Eros lubricant** and a tiny vibrating Pocket Rocket™.

Back in the car, put something really hot on the stereo, and crank it up. Keep the blanket within reach! You never know when she might need it. Now drive – and stroke her. Put a little oil on your fingers and plunge them between her exposed lips; rub them *zip zip zip* across her clit. At a stoplight, get out the little vibrator and tease her with it. Press it firmly into her. Watch her face as she struggles to hide that deep flush of **arousal** from other drivers. Switch back and forth, buzzer to fingers and back again, while you take the Foreplay Express back to your house, your bedroom, your bed, where the loudest, fastest, biggest bang of your life is waiting.

This time, I suspect, you will be at *her* mercy.

"In my sex fantasy, nobody ever loves me for my mind."

-Nora Ephron

No Panties!

You're going on an Adventure

during which you will experience

Lust, Arousal, Stimulation

(both Mental and Physical),

and at least one head-spinning, thigh-clenching Climax.

But your host must have Free and Unfettered Access

to your Most Intimate Parts, and that means you must wear

A Skirt and

No Panties

Oh, and you _must_ bring a blanket.

Really. You'll need it.

Meet me:_____

On:_____

At:_____

R.S.V.P — Please take the panties you will _not_ be wearing

and place them on my pillow one morning this week.

52 Invitations to Grrreat Sex

n u m b e r 9

Kitty In Heat

For Her Eyes Only

"The tragedy is when you've got sex in the head instead of down where it belongs."

-D.H. Lawerence

n u m b e r 9

Kitty In Heat

i n g r e d i e n t s

- 1 shower
- 2 candles

- Razor and scissors (Gotta groom that kitty! Speaking of which: she might be a marathon champion... but your lover's tongue is going to need a couple of rest stops! Don't forget to let him catch his breath.)

He Brings:
1 kitchen timer
... and a little oral Viagra!

Have you ever wanted, just once, to have sex like a man?

No, I don't mean fast, and then off to sleep! I mean aggressive... dominant... strong. I mean that *you* are in control, and your pleasure comes first. In all the thousands of interviews I've conducted over the years, this keeps coming up as one of the top sexual fantasies of women - and men. Yes, it's true; men secretly love the idea of a woman in charge in the **bedroom**. This week, you're going to make that fantasy come true for both of you.

All over the world, there's one universal signal that a woman is seriously ready for seduction: a **well-trimmed kitty**. Use scissors and a razor to make your private little thatch of hair shorter and neater (or get rid of it altogether!)... but don't let your lover see your handiwork until the big night. Surprise, after all, is the essence of a really good seduction.

He'll already be surprised by your invitation, which asked him to bring a common kitchen timer. When you greet him at the bedroom door, take his little gift and set it aside - *"Oh, that's for later,"* you'll say. *"We're going to get plenty of use for it during the Marathon."* His **libido** will quickly heat up to the same fevered pitch as his curiosity when you you start to undress by the light of the two candles you have burning in the room. *"You, too. I want to watch you take your clothes off. And then I have a treat for you."*

Take one of the candles and lead him to the shower. Once the temperature is just right, blow out the candle and join him under the warm, **steamy spray**. The other candle should be left far enough away in the bedroom so that you're taking your shower in complete darkness. Take your time indulging in the sensual mystery of it all. Slip and slide and grab and stroke, and do it all by your sense of touch alone.

The one remaining candle will light your way back to the bed. Tell him lie down on his back. Tell him you've been dreaming about this next event all week. Tell him he's about to enter The Velvet Tongue Marathon. Not 26.4 miles, like a runners marathon - this one is for 26.4 *minutes*, and during that time he's going to lick you and suck you and use his tongue like never before. Ready? Set? Twist the knob on the timer... and *go*.

Climb right up on his face. And don't be shy - use your clitoris like a a man uses his penis. Push yourself into his mouth. Gently roll your hips up and back, up and back, as if riding a trotting horse... or a **throbbing erection**. Reward him with moans of pleasure; there's nothing that turns a man on more than knowing he's giving his mate a sexual thrill. Encourage him - *"Oh, yes, that's it... oh, that's so good. Oh, wow, you know just how to make me so hot. Oh, God, please don't stop...."*

Not that you would even *let* him stop. Oh, no. For every one of your 26.4 minutes, you're going to explore every possible way to put your very wet kitty in contact with his tongue. Turn around and ride his mouth. Roll onto your side, wrap your legs around his head, and **squeeze him** into you. Kneel at the edge of the bed - not on your hands and knees, or even your elbows and knees, but in the far more enticing and erotic position described in the Kama Sutra: your face and breasts pressed to the bed, your beautiful, inviting bottom in the air. Demand that he kneel behind you and suck. Oh, and please, use that word; tell him to suck you and eat you; use the darkest, naughtiest language you know. The more forceful and commanding you are, the more insanely aroused he'll become.

Which will probably make for a really short return trip. Because, of course, once the timer goes off, you're going to reset it and invite him to participate in *your* version of the Velvet Tongue **Marathon**. But can he possibly last the whole 26.4 minutes?

Not if you've done your job right!

"The tragedy is when you've got sex in the head instead of down where it belongs."

-D.H. Lawerence

On your Mark. Get Hot.

Go!

An evening of

Exceptionally Erotic Bedroom Athletics

which will test the limits of your ability to receive

(and give)

Sexual Pleasure

awaits you at the start of

The Marathon.

You are required to bring a very open mind and

One Kitchen Timer

When:_____

Where:_____

Why: Because your hostess has been dreaming of nothing

else for an entire week.

R.S.V.P. by delivering five kiss ups.

That's a push-up... on top of me... with a kiss at the bottom

of every stroke.

52 Invitations to Grrreat Sex

n u m b e r 10

Silver Tongued-Devil

FOR HIS EYES ONLY

"All really great lovers are articulate, and verbal seduction is the surest road to actual seduction"

-Marya Mannes

n u m b e r 1O

Silver Tongued-Devil

i n g r e d i e n t s

- Paper (Boner, uh, *bonus* points if it's really elegant and beautiful. Parchment, for instance, or hand-made paper, wrapped in ribbon. Hint: practice on the cheap stuff first!)

- Words (C'mon, you can do it. Just say what you felt the first time you got under her clothes. Then again, these pages are sealed. If you just copy the ones I gave you, she'll never know the difference – and you'll get all the credit!)
- Candles

She Brings
High heels
Shoebox
Her box

Do you practice aural sex?

Not *oral* sex. Of course you practice that! And practice and practice, I hope. I mean aural, as in *listening with your ears*. I can guarantee that your lover does it. Words have a powerful effect on women. Just look at what turns us on: men look at pictures; women read erotica.

This week you're going to create a tiny masterpiece of erotic literature that stars your very own lover. You're going to pour out your heart in a *sex letter*. Make it hot. Use the kind of words you would never utter in public, the kind reserved strictly for your sweetie's ears. And if you have a hard time thinking of your own, start with these:

Do you know how much you turn me on? A dozen times a day I think of you, and feel a stirring between my legs. I sit at work, busy as ever, and suddenly see an image of you stepping out of the shower, hair glistening, skin glowing, and I have to hide my all-too-visible **arousal**. *You probably think your jeans are plain and casual, but to me they are sexier than anything; every time I see you in them I want to throw you on the bed and tug down that zipper and slide my hand down the front, fingers trapped between rough fabric and hot skin.*

I worship your breasts. They're perfect. Oh, I know you don't think so, but to me they are the finest in creation, worthy of praise. Have you caught me staring at them? I do, you know. I can see them through every bra, every blouse; I know those incredible nipples better than I know myself. My secret wish: that you would show them to me every single morning before I leave.

You probably don't know that I want to climb under every dress you've ever worn. So polite I have to be, so gentlemanly in public, but your hemline swirls with every step, teasing me, arousing me until I want to bend you over the sofa, throw your skirt up over your hips, **rip your panties away** *and plunge my* **throbbing erection** *into you. Even as I write this, the thought of your beautiful bare cheeks, so open and inviting, makes my heart race... and my cock grow.*

I adore your pussy. I love the taste of it, the feel of it. I love the way your sweet cunny lips swell up against my mouth and your clit comes out to greet me when it's happy. I could spend, oh, God, endless hours lapping up your juices. I confess: I want you to fuck my mouth. Yes I do, just like this — I want you to sit on my chest, straddle my face and push your **sopping wet puss** *into my mouth; I want you to ride my tongue as long as you need to, as long as you can, until you scream and collapse, unable to move. When we're ninety, I will still want your tired old bones cuddled next to mine, bare-ass naked in the same warm bed. I love you. I am consumed by you.*

Ohmigosh. Just writing this has made me wet. Trust me, your lover's panties will be soaked by the time she finishes this letter of yours.

She's bringing her sexiest high heels to your big date, still in a shoebox. Ask her to put them on while she reads your letter by candlelight. Keep them on while you make love. Talk dirty to her. Use the words and phrases from your letter; tell her exactly what you want, and what you're going to do to her. When it's all over, put the shoes back in the box, and slip the letter underneath. She'll never look at the box again without thinking of your passionate words. She'll never put those shoes on without rereading that scorching letter. She'll never wear them out of the house without first boinking you half to death.

Those expensive shoes are starting to look like a bargain, aren't they?

"All really great lovers are articulate, and verbal seduction is the surest road to actual seduction"

-Marya Mannes

Sex and High Heels

Do you have a pair of shoes that make you feel sexy?

Flirtatious? Saucy? Sultry? Cocky? Alluring?

Confident? Frisky? Seductive? Daring? Lusty?

When you put them on,

do you become ever so slightly

Wicked?

(If not — go buy some!)

Bring them to me — still in a shoebox

(The shoes are for fun. The box is for... well, you'll see....)

Place:_____

Date:_____

Time:_____

R.S.V.P. —To signal your acceptance of this invitation,

take my face in your hands, place it between your breasts,

and squeeze.

52 Invitations to Grrreat Sex

n u m b e r **I I**

Out Of The Ordinary,
And Into Her Pants $ $

FOR HIS EYES ONLY

"It's not the men in my life that count-it's the life in my men."

-Mae West

n u m b e r **II**

Out Of The Ordinary, And Into Her Pants

- 1 moving van
- 1 moving woman
- 1 perfect parking place
- Dinner for 2 (with whipped cream and other erotic edibles)
- Portable stereo

- Ice chest
- Matches (for her candles)
- Duct tape
- Blankets and pillows
- Folding table and chairs (optional)

She Brings
2 candles
2 candle holders
1 smiling, hungry mouth, ready for you to fill

Sometimes, the only difference between sex and *grrreat* sex... is the location! You don't think thousands of couples go to thousands of B&B's every weekend for the *breakfast,* do you? Uh-uh. The whole hospitality industry boils down to two segments: business travel, and what a friend of mine in the hotel business laughingly calls the "**soak-and-poke**" trade. (It took me a second to get it, too – think "Jacuzzi!")

You don't need a luxury hotel suite. (Well, okay, you do need one, but that's another seduction!) To make sex more fun and exciting, you just need to occasionally do it someplace other than your bed. **Someplace unusual**. Someplace like...well, like the back of a moving van.

I don't mean an eighteen-wheel tractor-trailer rig. No, I'm suggesting you go rent a Ryder, the kind you can get for $29.95 a day. A bargain, if you ask me; that's less than the cost of a hotel, or dinner and a movie. And your mate will never be able to accuse you of being predictable – not after you pick her up for a date in one of these bob-tail babies!

Her curiosity, which has been simmering since she got your invitation, is now at a full boil. What's in the back of that thing? Why did your invitation request a pair of candles? And where the heck are you going? Don't give anything away; just chat and drive until you reach your destination. Where that is depends on where you live, but what it has is this: a really fabulous view. Mountains? Ocean? City lights? Whatever you choose, park facing away from the scenery. Ask her to wait a moment. Then grab her candles, jump in the back, and set up your **surprise**.

It's dinner *á deux,* picked up from a really nice restaurant and set out on a big blanket – or better yet, a folding table and chairs. Your mobile picnic affords the best view of the sunset, and at least some of the comforts of home. Your boombox fills the air with music, while your ice chest keeps the drinks properly chilled. And that sliding door provides more privacy than most campers ever get when it's time for, um, **private** things.

Speaking of which – get out your duct tape and cover the hole where the door latch goes. You do *not* want to find yourselves accidentally locked in! But if you're feeling a little brave (and a lot wicked), you might want to consider the Laura Corn Exhibitionist-At-Heart option: *leave the door open.*

Pile up your pillows and bury your lover under some blankets. Turn the dinner table over on it's side; it makes a nice screen if she wants a place to hide. Now for the real meal deal: a dab of whipped cream crowning each breast like snow on mountains. Almost too pretty to eat, huh? Two long, slow slurps will leave her nipples clean and wet and standing at attention. She'll **giggle** when you line up little cubes of Jell-O™ on her tummy, but the laughs will melt into moans as you nibble your way down, lower... and lower... and oh, my, there's a perfect spot for another shot of Cool Whip. Lap it up, and take your time. By now, of course, she's developed an appetite of a different sort. And by now your special dessert is more than ready to be unzipped from the oven.

Yes, something with a cream-filled center ought to really hit the spot. Mmm-mm!

"It's not the men in my life that count-it's the life in my men.

-Mae West

Dinner and other
Pleasures of the Flesh Await

and quite possibly, if the tip is large enough,

All at the Same Time

The Restaurant which will be Hosting our Meal

has a simple and singular Dress Code:

Clothing must be designed for

Easy Access

(or at least Easily Removable!)

You are asked only to bring An Appetite

(For dinner as well as other delights)

and a Pair of Candles, in Holders

Prepare to depart on: _____ evening

at _____ o'clock

Any contact this week between Your Lips and My Body

will constitute your R.S.V.P.

52 Invitations to Grrreat Sex

n u m b e r **12**

Slave Me

For Her Eyes Only

*"What do men really want? Erotic variety.
He wants something other than a dozen roses and
a love note on his pillow."*

-Susan Crain Bakos

n u m b e r **I 2**

Slave Me

i n g r e d i e n t s

- Candles
- Cushions
- Note
- Very short see-through nightie

- Black felt-tip pen. (You might want to practice with chalk first, but it's surprisingly easy to write on your own butt. Oh, I'll never forget the moment Jeff saw those words on my cheeks. It was the beginning of some of the greatest sex of my life – once he remembered to start breathing! So what if it doesn't wash off right away? To me, that's a plus!)

He Brings:
Black stockings
Wicked thoughts

"*I* hope you're ready for the ride of your life Saturday night...."

That's what you'll whisper in your lover's ear one day this week... and for maximum impact, I suggest you do it when he's not alone. *"Maybe it's this book I've been reading... maybe it's the weather, I don't know... but I've just been so-o-o-ooo* **horny** *lately. I'm aching for you."*

Is that a little out of character for you? That's exactly the point of this week's seduction. You're going to unleash a side of you that – unless he's one hell of a lucky guy – he may have only fantasized about before. You're going to be a very bad girl for him. And men lo-o-oove bad girls.

"Oh, wow, I dreamed about you last night. I dreamed you were doing it to me at the mall, right in front of everybody, and... oh, gosh, I'm so wet! Here, feel this... no, that's enough, we've got to get ready for work..."

Tease him like that every day this week. No matter how long you've been together, no matter how old he is, he'll be howling like a tomcat one fence away from a kitty in heat. Call him at his office: *"I just don't know what's gotten into me, honey. I keep thinking about having you in my mouth again...."*

By Saturday, his blood will be boiling with the **pent-up lust** of a thousand men. He'll be able to think of nothing but you. (And isn't that the reason you bought this book? Here's one of the secrets to keeping your relationship hot: every week, let him know you crave him so much that you just can't control yourself. You'll be amazed at what that does to his self-esteem. And his erection.)

And now, it's time to send him over the top; time to show him that you're all the bad girl he'll ever need. You're going to be wilder than his most wicked fantasies. For one night... *you're going to be his* **sexual slave**.

Your invitation asked him to bring a pair of seamed nylon stockings, and no doubt he's thinking they'll go on on his favorite pair of legs – but he's wrong. When he arrives at the door, he sees a room lit up with candles, a lovely woman in a slinky gown... and a pile of sofa cushions on the floor. Without saying a word, you kiss him, and hand him a note. *"The stockings?"* it reads. *"I want you to use them to tie me up."*

Now shrug off the robe, put your wrists together in front, and wait while his poor little overloaded brain catches up. At this point, he may have trouble remembering how to tie a knot! Turn and, ever so slowly, walk to the cushions. Kneel on them. As you bend forward to place your bound wrists and elbows on the floor, it becomes clear that there are no panties beneath your sexy little nightie... ah, but there's more than just bare flesh. In the flickering glow he can make out a message; words scribbled in black felt-tip ink across your suggestively **upthrust bottom**, one on each rosy cheek...

Slave. Me.

For the rest of the evening, you are an obedient sexual servant. Speak when spoken to and perform on command. Every caress is greeted by a moan; every stroke met with a squeal of unadulterated pleasure. Each gasp and groan and *yes-baby-yes-do-it-harder-do-it-<u>harder</u>* will help him unleash the wild sexual animal within. And take it from me, those are the very best kinds of animals to keep around the house.

Once they're properly trained, of course. And isn't that the other reason why you bought this book?

"What do men really want? Erotic variety. He wants something other than a dozen roses and a love note on his pillow."

-Susan Crain Bakos

Hello, Sailor!
Want a Cookie?

Your Ship Has Come In

and your Welcome Home party is at _____

this _____ *night*

starting at _____ *o'clock sharp.*

Be prepared for an evening of

Debauchery

Sensual Thrills

and Extreme Gratitude expressed in shockingly sexual ways

The price of admission is:

One Pair Of Black Nylons

(The kind with the seam up the back!)

R.S.V.P. any morning this week by placing several kisses exactly where you

think that seam will go.

52 Invitations to Grrreat Sex

number **13**

What Every Woman Should
Do For The Man She Loves

For Her Eyes Only

"The passion and starry-eyed joys of the honeymoon are but callow experiments in a search for the magnificent which lies beyond the horizon."

-Barbara Cartland, British romantic novelist

number 13

What Every Woman Should Do For The Man She Loves

ingredients

- 1 totally confident woman
- 1 completely professional masseuse
- 1 perfectly timed arrival (Your masseuse should set up while your lover is in the shower. She can wait in the lobby for your phone call.)
- 1 robe for him
- 1 flower shop
- 1 hotel room

- candles, lots
- lingerie, sexy
- lubricant, slick (You've *got* to try Eros™ – "Europe's #1 Moisturizing Lubricant." I just love it!)
- music, soft. (Those CDs with ocean or rain sounds would work well. My choice? A quiet, sexy disc called "Jazz For A Rainy Afternoon.")

He Brings:
1 rose
1 very big smile!

*H*ave you ever had sex that was so great you were still talking about it weeks later? Has it ever been so great that you wanted to call your *friends* and tell them about it?

You will. And this is the one that will do it. It's big, memorable, and yes, a little expensive, depending on how you set it up. But remember, you only have to do something like this once or twice a year. On his birthday or Father's Day, or even for no special reason at all, this kind of seduction sends a powerful message to your mate. This one says that he's the most important thing in your life, that he's *worth* pulling out all the stops for. For one night, you're going demonstrate the depth of your feelings for him in the most physical and intimate of ways.

I suggest you do it on a Friday evening. That's when he's exhausted from a week of work, I'll bet, and trying hard to put his job out of his mind. This week, though, your invitation will put something entirely different in his head! He may be tired and a little ragged, he'll sure be **excited** when he gets to the hotel suite you've rented, carrying the single red rose you asked him to bring.

The sensual assault begins the moment you open the door. The room is lit only by the glow of two dozen candles... or better yet, a fireplace. Your fragrance draws him in. A makeover shows your face in a lovely new way, and your **sexy lace** nightgown hints at pleasures to come. Greet him with a hug, and warm words of welcome: *"Oh, sweetie, I've been looking forward to this for days...."*

Encourage him to take a shower. By the time he's through, your special guest will have arrived: *a professional masseuse,* carrying her own portable massage table. Please don't be embarrassed to arrange this treat; these are not "working girls" but trained professionals, and they will not perform any act that is even remotely sexual. Ah, but the kind of magic they *can* create is... almost indescribable. The tension melts out of your mate's muscles as she digs deep into his back. The stress of the week is washed away by **waves of bliss**. He's left with an overwhelming sense of awe that you did this for him.

Only after your masseuse has left does the evening become more sensual. Give your man a drink and some hors d'ouvres, and encourage him to talk about his day. Then grab his hand and lead him to bed. *"I couldn't help but notice that our friend kept missing a very important spot."* Get out a bottle of lotion; I recommend a product called Eros™. *"There's this one little muscle that didn't get the rubdown it deserves. Would you like me to finish the massage?"*

Yes, yes, ohhh, *yes,* he would. Coat his growing manhood liberally with lotion. Focus all your attention on it; make it the center of your universe. Pull it, and stroke it. Wrap your hands around it, one above the other, and gently twist in opposite directions. Make a fist right above the throbbing tip and push down, slowly opening your fingers as the **firm flesh** slides past your palm, then immediately do the same with your other hand, and repeat. Use your fingers to form a ring around his shaft, then – *fast! and hard!* – pull up and down, up and down, adding lotion as needed, until you feel the countdown beginning. He swells even more, he gasps for air, his muscles clench, his buttocks practically rise off the bed, and finally...

Blastoff.

And the evening has only just begun....

"*The passion and starry-eyed joys of the honeymoon are but callow experiments in a search for the magnificent which lies beyond the horizon.*"

-Barbara Cartland, British romantic novelist

You make me Hot

You make me Wet. You make my nipples hard and my toes curl.

In my Heart and Soul and between my Legs,

I get a rush of Pleasure when I think that

You are Mine

And to prove it, I am going to treat you to an evening of

Unbridled Lust and
Unparalleled Sensuality

the likes of which you have never seen, and will never forget.

Your Instructions:

This _____ evening at _____ pm,

you are to visit a flower shop called

_____

and pick up a

single red rose

Bring it to me at _____ pm Sharp.

I will be waiting, nearly nude and more than ready, at

_____

Don't come late.

(But come often!)

52 Invitations to Grrreat Sex

n u m b e r 14

Sensual Assault $$$

FOR HIS EYES ONLY

Watch sex. It is the key to success and the trap door to failure.

-Michael Shea

n u m b e r **14**

Sensual Assault

i n g r e d i e n t s

- Roses. Lots of roses. (And here's a tip: you only need one perfect long-stemmed rose. The ones you tear apart can be the shorter, thornier, and much less expensive kind. Shop around)
- White lingerie, giftwrapped
- Polaroid camera and film
- Hotel room, optional

She Brings:
Long scarf for blindfold
Her own little bud...
... in the Garden of Eatin'!

*P*lease don't take this personally – but men just don't seem to get the Rule Of Flowers.

The Rule is this: You get Romance Points for flowers only if your sweetheart doesn't *expect* flowers. A bouquet sent to her office? A handful of lilies "just because?" Big score!

But handing your lover flowers at a time when you're *supposed* to do so... well, sorry. No points for you. (Oh, but just try to get away with *no* flowers on her birthday! My friend, you'll be digging your way out of Romance Debt for weeks to come.)

I've come up with a way to bend the Rule, though. You're going to give your sweetie flowers on Valentine's Day, just like every man is supposed to – but you're going to do it in such a surprising, special way that her girlfriends will all be wishing they had *you* in their lives.

You'll need roses. Lots of roses. They can be especially expensive around Valentine's Day, but this seduction can work just as well for any other significant occasion. And you'll need some slinky, sexy white lingerie, nicely wrapped, of course. Here's a Laura Corn tip: don't immediately pick out the tiniest thing in the store! You know your mate pretty well. Does she really like to wear **itty-bitty skin-revealing** lapdance outfits? Or is she more comfortable in a demure teddy? This treat is for *her*, remember, so pick out something she'll love to wear.

The night of **your seduction**, meet her just outside your bedroom – or your hotel room, if your budget permits. Your invitation instructed her to bring a *long silk scarf*, which you will gently tie around her head to cover her eyes. You'll see a smile spread across her face when you hand her your giftwrapped package. And now, lead her through the door into your specially prepared boudoir.

She can unwrap the gift herself, but she'll need your help to put it on – and do I really need to point out how much fun that will be? Lead her to the bed and ask her to lay down. Watch her reaction as she realizes *she's stretching out on hundreds of fragrant rose petals*, torn from the blossoms and scattered across the sheets. **Her skin** has never felt anything quite like the so-very-soft touch of the petals, from her head to her toes. The scent is almost overwhelming, sending signals of love and **lust** with every breath.

Take a single long-stemmed rose, petals still intact, and begin to paint her body. Start by caressing her face with the flower. Glide it along her shoulders, down past her breasts, pausing only to place a single petal over each nipple. Scatter more of the blossom across her tummy, **thighs and hips** as you trace your way down to her secret garden.

Now for a special treat: remove her blindfold and let her see the proverbial bed of roses come to life. Shower her with more petals, like a ruby-red snowfall, then commemorate the sheer beauty of the moment with a Polaroid camera. (Don't forget Laura's Rule Of Naughty Pictures: *Always* give the prints to the woman, to keep or destroy as she wishes!)

Finally, it's time to concentrate on *her* little blossom – the one that's now blooming between her thighs. "A rose by any other name would smell as sweet," Shakespeare wrote.

And none in the world can match *this* one for taste!

"Watch sex. It is the key to success and the trap door to failure."

-Michael Shea

Come One! Come All!
To The Red & White Ball

at which an entirely new form of

Sensual Stimulation and Erotic Enjoyment

will be explored, using volunteers from the audience,

which consists entirely of

_____ and _____

Caution: This special event features adult content.

Guests who do not wish to receive

Intimate Physical Contact and Many Wonderful Orgasms

are requested to decline.

Those who choose to accept are asked to bring

This Invitation and

One Long Silk Scarf

To: _____

On: _____

At: _____

Dress code: irrelevant

Costume will be provided

52 Invitations to Grrreat Sex

n u m b e r 15

Invitation to Sin

FOR HIS EYES ONLY

Be a good animal, true to your animal instincts.

-D.H. Lawrence

n u m b e r 15

Invitation to Sin

i n g r e d i e n t s

• One candle
• One match
• Lotion (if necessary)

• Several flattering photos
• Absolutely no fear

She Brings:
One kitchen chair

Are you ready for something different? Something that's maybe a little bit... *nasty?*

This week you're going to share a secret with your lover. You're going to show her something you've never let anyone see before, *ever.* The idea of opening yourself up like this might scare you at first, but perhaps I can put your mind at ease by pointing out two things.

One, sexual secrets are an absolutely over-the-top, weak-at-the-knees, clit-throbbing *thrill.* There's hardly anything that binds a couple better than a truly wicked private fantasy that blows your minds every time you indulge in it. You thought it was only men who felt that way? Uh-uh. Point number two – *women dig it.* Our erotica doesn't usually have pictures like yours, but it's easily as **intense**. Those romance novels aren't just kisses and torn bodices.

Your mate's voyage into uncharted territory begins when she greets you at your bedroom door, carrying the kitchen chair you requested in your invitation. The room is nearly dark, with only a single candle casting a flickering glow. Set the chair in a corner and make sure she's comfortable in it. Give her a good **long kiss**, then whisper, *"No talking. Only silence."* Now blow out the candle. The next part of the show is **for her ears only**.

She can hear the rustling of the sheets as you settle onto the bed. She hears... what? Objects being moved, paper shuffling, *something.* And then a soft, subtle noise begins. Barely perceptible at first, but its **steady rhythm** makes it intriguing. Is it getting louder? Uhh... yes, and so is your **breathing**. Her mind races; her imagination takes off. She's certain there's something highly sexual going on here, just out of reach of her senses. It's turning her on, and she's burning with curiosity. Suddenly it stops. What's happening? What's he doing? What's going on?

She hears the *scritch* of a match being lit, watches the spark as it moves to the candle. She sees that her erotic imagination was on target – oh, wow, you've been *playing with yourself,* tugging on your penis, making it **hard and huge**. She's mesmerized by the sight, by the very thought of it. And then she notices:

You're surrounded by pictures. There's one in your free hand, and you're gazing at it while you **slowly stroke** your erection. And the photo... all the photos... are of her. Not Playboy, not Penthouse – *her.* You cannot underestimate the impact of this stunning scene. It will forever erase any doubt that *she's* the one who turns you on. Oh, she's way past her boundaries now. She's seeing the wild, carnal side of men that no woman ever sees, but all suspect exists. And it's making her *very* hot.

Let her watch a while longer. Let her see the steam building in you as you creep up on an orgasm. Then clear away some of her portraits and invite her over. Take her hand, and place it over your cock. Guide it. Wrap your fingers around hers and show her exactly how to do it – the right speed, the right pressure. *Teach her to masturbate you.* She won't be able to take her eyes off the **throbbing** slab in her hand. You, however, should watch her face. See her expression move from wide-eyed fascination to focused concentration, from blushing excitement to the beaming glow of look-what-I-did *pride* as creamy white jets of jism pour over her hand and onto your belly....

And then her face takes on a look that can only be described as *horny.* Too bad Mr. Stiffy's going to be out of commission for the next several minutes. Ah, but your tongue isn't! Put it to good use. As my Grandpa used to say, there's more than one way to skin a cat – although he wasn't talking about this particular kind of pussy!

At least, I don't think so. But then, Grandma always used to blush the deepest shade of red when he said it... hmm....

"Be a good animal, true to your animal instincts."

-D.H. Lawrence

Dark Secrets

that reside in the wickedest, most sexual part

of the Human Psyche

Will Be Revealed

During a special evening of Debauchery and

Erotic Fantasies Come True

Are you Brave Enough to Face It?

Do you feel Compelled to Explore the Naughty Side of

your Mind?

Then bring One Kitchen Chair to the Bedroom

at precisely _____ o'clock

this _____ night

No late seating will be permitted.

52 Invitations to Grrreat Sex

n u m b e r 16

Make Me $

For Her Eyes Only

Men play the game: women know the score

-Roger Waddis

number 16

Make Me

ingredients

- Several outfits that allow for easy flashing
- 1 clever man
- 1 flirtatious woman
- 1 bit of advice: clear your calender. And your bedroom!

*I*f you've heard one of my radio shows, then you're probably already aware of my Magic Formula. It's an essential ingredient in every loving relationship, and it's at the core of every seduction in all of my books:

Anticipation plus Variety equals Total Excitement.

Everyone understands the variety part. When a relationship is just beginning, your lover is full of surprises. Every week is a different date, every trip takes you to an unknown place. Sadly, variety is one of the first things that fades as a relationship matures and you get to know each other well, in the bedroom and in the rest of your lives. And as I said, everyone gets it. It's easy to recognize a rut when you're in it. Lucky for me, of course! That's what usually inspires people to buy my books.

Ah, but anticipation is a hidden quality. It's not a thing; it's a feeling, and when it goes away, it can be hard to say what's missing. But you can sure feel its power when it comes back! When your lover hints that he has a treat for you, what he's really saying is that he thinks enough of you to plan ahead. When he **teases** you about secret plans for an upcoming date, he's telling you that you're never far from his mind. It flat-out feels *great* to know that he doesn't take you for granted. It's fun to have something to look forward to.

Oh, and there's the hot sex angle, too. Nothing like two or three days of **foreplay** to put you in the mood for some skin time!

This week's seduction is all about anticipation. Seventy-two hours worth, starting from the time your mate gets his invitation. It's an unusual one, as you can see; it seems to put all the burden on him. You're challenging him to come up with something new and **thrilling and exciting** for you. It only looks like you've got the week off, though – because while he's planning and scheming, you're going to be teasing and flirting. Show him how much he turns you on. Convince him that his efforts will result in a *really* big reward. Tease him! And do it in a way even the densest guy couldn't miss.

In the morning, don't just pop out of bed – roll across him so that your breasts slide over his face. When he's in the shower, open the curtain and give him wet kiss... and a wet stroke. *"Hmm... forty-eight hours!"* When he gets home, turn your hug into a sensual moment; pull open his shirt, and then lift yours, so that your bare nipples press against his chest. *"Oooh, thirty-six hours, honey! I can hardly wait."* Flash him throughout the week! A bit of bare bottom here, an **exposed breast** there. *"Twenty-four hours to go..."*

Unless this is the way you always behave – and he's one lucky son-of-a-gun if you do! – then these overtures are going to light a fire under him. He's going to see you in a whole new light.... or rather, the same light that shone on you when he first met you. That was the **glow** of *anticipation,* a look that convinced him you held the key to an unknown universe of possibilities. Remember: Anticipation plus Variety equals Total Excitement. You're giving this guy a month's worth of anticipation in just seventy-two hours! In return, he's going to knock himself out to come up with a nice surprise for you.

And what of his surprise just isn't... well, surprising enough? Don't you dare let him suspect, or he won't be likely to try again. Time to use another Laura Corn Magic Formula – my Recipe For Building Better Lovers:

Fake It 'til you Make It!

"Men play the game: women know the score."

-Roger Waddis

Are you Man Enough to Take the Challenge?

Your Goal, should you accept, is to come up with

something completely

New

Dream up something exciting, something arousing, something we've never done before. In other words:

Make Me!

Make me hot. Make me be bad. Make me want to give you

Sexual Favors, Erotic Treats

and at least one knee-shaking, butt-clenching,

bounce-off-the-ceiling Orgasm. And More.

However

You have only 72 Hours to work your magic,

beginning from the moment you acknowledge receipt of this Invitation by

planting a Kiss on my Lips while whispering "The Clock Is Ticking."

Time and Place is up to You. Your Reward is up to Me!

52 Invitations to Grrreat Sex

n u m b e r **17**

Good Girls Go To Heaven But
Bad Girls Go *Everywhere* $ $

For Her Eyes Only

'What do you call a bad man?'
'The sort of man who admires innocence.'
'And a bad woman?'
"Oh, the sort of woman a man never gets tired of."

-Anonymous

n u m b e r **17**

Good Girls Go To Heaven But Bad Girls Go *Everywhere*

i n g r e d i e n t s

- Thigh strap (Like the "Thigh One On," available in fabric or leather. If you don't see it at your local adult boutique, call Good Vibrations™ ats 1-800-289-8423)
- Dildo (The base must be wider than the shaft, so the strap can hold it)
- Giftwrapped box, to deliver the toy to your lover
- Bottle of Eros™, or other premium lubricant
- Mirror

He Brings
Two penises – one real, one faux, both fun!

When I started doing research for this book, I opened up the Good Vibrations™ catalog and ordered... oh, everything. (Imagine explaining to your tax accountant that your business expenses for the year included printer paper, stamps – *and a big box of vibrators!*) Sure, experimenting with dozens of outfits and gadgets designed to enhance your sexual experience may seem like tough, grueling work, but I just had to do it. For the book, you know. Hey, I did it for *you*.

I was really intrigued by one especially sexy item in the shipment – and as always, the Good Vibes support staff was more than happy to explain how it worked. It's called a *thigh strap-on*. It's a small, wide belt with Velcro at each end, and a hole in the middle that's just **big** enough to securely hold a dildo. No, not one of those S&M monsters you might have seen in bad movies, but a cute, squishy little silicone model, in a size that won't intimidate you or your man. Wrap it and send it to your lover with orders to bring it, still sealed, to your big date.

From the moment you greet him at the door, your attitude should make it clear that this is not an ordinary evening. You are in charge tonight. You are **hot**, and you will not be denied. Kiss him. Undress him. Then ask him to open his gift... and put it on.

He'll be stunned, I'll bet. This is naughty; this is *nasty*, the kind of thing guys fantasize about, but think women don't. Tonight, you are every man's most secret erotic dream. You're a *cock addict*, an absolute junky for penetration, and you're going to demonstrate your helpless craving in the most graphic way possible. Have him sit up on the edge of the bed. Slip the dildo through the opening in the belt, then fasten the strap around his thigh so that the toy is **straight up**, in parallel with his own rising flesh. Slather it with a safe lubricant. Face him while you straddle his leg... and watch his eyes pop when you lower yourself onto the toy.

Rock, and roll, and slither up and down. And don't neglect the real thing between his legs; stroke it with your hand while you ride his second **erection**. How many ways can you show off your lust? Try this: make him lay on his tummy, with a mirror positioned so that he can see both of you. Slide the strap around so that the dildo is pointing up again, and play with his bottom while you writhe on his thigh. Pull the toy from the strap and slip it between his cheeks; he'll be hypnotized by the sight of you bouncing up and down on his bare butt.

The ultimate erotic moment, the one that will be seared into his sexual memory forever, begins when you make him turn over... and place the base of the toy in his mouth. Ask him to hold it while you lower yourself onto his face. This is a staggering, mind-shattering, intensely erotic image for him. He's getting to watch something he never sees, not this close: his favorite little kitty, hungrily devouring her favorite meal. *"Mmm, I've got another job for that mouth of yours,"* you'll tell him, as you slide back an inch or so. *"Hold the toy in me... and lick me at the same time. Go on, be a good boy. Eat me.* **Ohhhh, yeah**, *suck me, just like that...."*

Don't forget about his own aching organ. Turn around, slide your lips down his shaft, and let your mind run wild. In one end, you've got your lover's throbbing, twitching rod, and in the other you've got... well, *any man you can imagine*. Trust me, he won't complain about sharing you like this.

Men are funny that way. They can't talk when your mouth is full.

'What do you call a bad man?'
'The sort of man who
admires innocence.'
'And a bad woman?'
"Oh, the sort of woman a man
never gets tired of."

-Anonymous

Do Not Open

unless you are hot and bothered and fully erect and naked and minutes

away from an explosive, scrotum-scrunching toe-curling orgasm and

Until I Say So.

Which will happen shortly after you bring this box – still sealed! – to:

_____

this _____ *evening*

at _____ *o'clock*

If you can come (more than once, I hope), please

R.S.V.P.

with a ten minute surprise foot massage any day this week.

If not, well, you will never learn the mystery behind the contents of

The Box. "Strong enough for a Man . . . yet Made for a Woman . . ."

52 Invitations to Grrreat Sex

n u m b e r 18

Hot Pursuit

FOR HIS EYES ONLY

*"Despite my thirty years of research into the feminine soul,
I have not yet been able to answer... the great question that has
never been answered: what does a woman want?"*

-Sigmund Freud

n u m b e r 18

Hot Pursuit

i n g r e d i e n t s

- Several cassette tapes (as many as you have destinations)
- Bath & Body Works (or something similar) and a few gifts
- Lingerie store, holding a gift-wrapped teddy
- Bakery, for dessert
- Other destinations: Flower shop? Bookstore? Adult Boutique?

- Hotel room
- Dinner

Special note: If her best friend can't go, then leave the first cassette in an envelope taped to the bathroom mirror or some other obvious place.

Bonus Points: Give her friend a camera to take pictures of this big adventure!

Budget tip: In the end, direct her back to your own clean and candle-lit house.

She Brings:
1 toothbrush
1 cassette player
1 amazed friend who will tell the world about the luckiest girl on Earth.

"*Well, we're playing a game, sort of, from this cool new book we bought. And it's <u>really sexy</u>!* I mean, look at this invitation I got in the mail! I can't wait to see what he's got planned."

That's your sweetheart, talking to her best friend. She keeps an eye on the door, looking for you – this is the right time, and the right restaurant, after all – but you're nowhere to be seen. It's a nice coincidence that her girlfriend just happened to be there. (Or is it?) *"And look at this... he asked me to bring a tape recorder! I can't imagine why."*

"Oh, I can," her friend replies, as she pulls out the cassette you secretly slipped her early in the week. *"We're supposed to listen to it, both of us, and follow the instructions!"* A moment of shock passes, a roaring laugh follows, and then they slide the tape into the machine and press "Start" on the greatest **romantic** adventure of the year; part Mission Impossible, part Wheel Of Fortune.

With music in the background, your recorded voice explains that many **wondrous** and special things await, beginning with their first stop: Bath & Body Works, in the mall, where the manager is waiting for them.

The staff at B&BW is already excited, since they heard about your treat when you set it up the day before. The girls at the counter grin and hand over your gift, which includes three things – a bottle of deliciously scented **massage oil** for your sweetheart, an elegant little bar of milled soap for her friend (with a nice thank-you-for-your-help message attached)... and another cassette tape! They'll all be squealing with excitement when they hear your next recorded message: *"How would you like to spend the evening being cherished and worshipped and adored by the man who loves you?"* Ooh! Ahh! The audience is very impressed, and your mate is beaming. *"Your next surprise, and more instructions, are waiting just down the mall at Victoria's Secret."*

Another package (and several excited saleswomen) are ready and waiting. Inside the box is a **sexy satin** teddy... and another cassette tape. *"I have candles burning, and music playing, and wine chilling. All that's missing ... is you. Oh, and <u>dessert</u>. Pick out your favorite at Foard's on Fourth Avenue, and then come see me. I miss you."*

Let's face it – you are becoming a legend in your home town. Everywhere these two friends go, people are learning about your **spectacular seduction**, and envying your lucky mate. Feel free to send her to a few more places; remember, as long as there's a treat and another cassette waiting at each stop, these girls are having a blast. The final tape includes directions to your hotel suite.

Needless to say, this is where the best friend departs, and the **real fun** begins. After she tells you about all the fun and excitement they had today, smile... and hand her one more tape. *"We have dinner reservations at eight,"* the recording says. *"Until then, how would you like to have a massage with that lotion you picked up today? Yes? Then go ahead and get undressed.... You don't mind if I sit here and watch, do you?"*

Hmmm... maybe you're going to be just a little bit late to dinner!

*"Despite my thirty years
of research into the feminine soul,
I have not yet been able
to answer...the great question
that has never been answered:
what does a woman want?"*

-Sigmund Freud

You are about to embark upon

A Thrilling and Heart-Racing True Life Adventure

during which you will find —

Romantic Surprises

Sensual Surprises

& Really Big, Tons-of-Fun,
I-Can't-Believe-My-Eyes Surprises

(All that and Dinner, too!)

This ride is for Adults Only,
and departs from _____
this _____ evening
at _____ o'clock

Please bring the following items:

one toothbrush
one cassette tape player

R.S.V.P. within 24 hours by leaving a pair of your perfumed
panties in the glove compartment of my car. You'll get them
back this weekend. (Whether you'll have time to put them
on is another question altogether.)

52 Invitations to Grrreat Sex

n u m b e r 19

Guilty of Everything $

FOR HIS EYES ONLY

Morality comes with the sad wisdom of age,
when the sense of curiosty has withered

-Graham Greene, British novelist

n u m b e r **19**

Guilty of Everything

i n g r e d i e n t s

- "His Secret Life," by Bob Berkowitz (with your favorite fantasies highlighted)
- "Women On Top," by Nancy Friday
- Giftwrapping for both books

- 1 purple highlighter
- 2 drinks
- 12 kisses

She Brings:
1 purple highlighter
2 red cheeks
1 wild imagination, soon to be unleashed

"*A* man's got to f*** my mind before he can f*** me." I've never heard it said better! It happened when a woman called one of my radio shows a few years back. In a dozen slightly-bleeped words, she summarized what dozens of authors have taken whole shelves of books to say:

Women dig fantasies. And if they don't, they should. Here's an amazing statistic – in a survey of a hundred thousand women, half admitted to having twice as much sex as the other half. And what did the **hot-blooded** half have in common?

Erotica. Yep, tales of love and lust and hot, sweaty sex. Women who read fantasies *have* fantasies, and much better sex lives. And wouldn't you just lo-o-oove to know what kinds of things make your **lover's panties** sopping wet?

Turn that around. Imagine the kind of lover she'd be if she knew what deep, nasty secrets *really* got your mojo working. Well, imagine no more, my friend; this week you're going to clue her in to the **secret fantasy** life of men.

You have Bob Berkowitz to thank for it. He's the former host of CNBC's sex show *Real Personal* and author of a book called "His Secret Life." This may turn out to be the best six and a half bucks you've ever spent. Bob has collected confessions from lots of men – all ages, all walks of life. These are true tales about their **hidden sexual thoughts**. And your lover is going to *love* them.

Go through the book with a bright purple highlighter and mark the titles of, oh, maybe ten confessions. Be sure to include at least one that's a fantasy of your own! I suggest heavy emphasis on the first chapter of the book, where Bob and his group candidly talk about the **hottest fantasy** of all, the *sexually aggressive woman*. Maybe you're already blessed with one, you lucky devil. But if she's the quiet kind who always lets you drive the Big Bang Bus, then this will give her all the encouragement she needs to occasionally grab the keys.

After a round of drinks and **laughs and kisses**, lead her to your book, neatly giftwrapped, waiting on the bed. *"I'll be back in ten minutes. Look it over; it's filled with... mmm, secrets. Sexual secrets. And,"* you might say with a wicked smile, *"I've marked some passages of particular interest...."*

Her mouth might still be wide open when you leave the room. *Holy cow, this is all about sex, guy sex, sex like my guy wants... ooooh, yeah!* She'll already be **warming up** by the time you come back. (Didn't I tell you this was a great investment??) Slide your hand between her thighs and you'll see what I mean. She may want to ask about the things she's read, and I encourage you to offer your critique... *while you're groping her.* Oh, this is my very favorite form of conversation – the kind where your mouth is always busy, even when you're listening. Talk, suck, talk, suck, orgasm, sigh.... What a happy world this would be if all our negotiations were handled this way.

If the Berkowitz book is the best bang for $6.50, then your other purchase has to be the greatest seven dollar investment of all time. Get Nancy Friday's collection of female fantasies called "Women On Top" and present it to your sweetie while you're both still in that delicious rosy can't-stop-smiling post-orgasmic glow. She already has her own highlighter – it was mentioned in your invitation – and she'll be more than happy to go through and mark her favorite passages for you to read next week. Make reservations for round two of your mutual talk-a-suck-athon.

And before your next erotic dialogue, don't be surprised if you're inspired to try a couple of, um, *monologues.* You get a rise out of those Penthouse letters? Wait until you see how hot these *women's* fantasies are. You're going to be sporting wood the size of Mark McGuire's bat!

"Morality comes with the sad wisdom of age, when the sense of curiosty has withered"

-Graham Greene, British novelist

Secrets

Naughty secrets. Sexual secrets. Unspeakable secrets.

There are a thousand mysteries to erotic love —

and you are invited to learn some of mine

this _____ evening

at _____ o'clock.

Meet me _____

and bring one

bright purple highlighter

R.S.V.P.

If one evening you take my hand,

guide it into your open robe and

lead my fingers to your own secret

spot...

... I'll take that as a "yes."

52 Invitations to Grrreat Sex

n u m b e r 2O

Pleasant Wet Dreams $

For Her Eyes Only

In one survey a thousand men were asked what turned them on most: dirty talk, x-rated videos, pornography, female masturbation, sexy lingerie, or "other." Of the men surveyed, 92% said they were most turned on by sexy lingerie. In an interesting footnote, 73% of these men said they relied on stimulation such as this to sustain their interest in a long-term relationship.

-Dr. Patricia Love

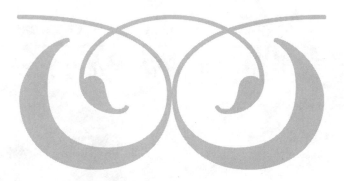

number 20

Pleasant Wet Dreams

ingredients

- Pulsing massage shower head (Special treat! Get a Vibra-Sponge™, a submersible vibrator encased in a sponge. Bath time will never be the same.)
- Stockings, garter belt, bra (The sexier, the better. Consider long gloves... and for a truly hot scene, get some of these items in latex or rubber!)

- Bonus points if you wear high heels. Sure, they'll be ruined. What the heck.
- Candles, beverages, music
- Towels. Lots and lots of towels.

No tub? No problem. The scorching image is you, wet, in lingerie and playing with a shower massage. It works just as well in a shower stall. (I know – I've done both!)

He Brings:
1 kitchen chair
2 hungry eyes

You *do* have a pulsing massage shower head, don't you? The kind with a long hose so you can lift out the sprayer and use it anywhere in the shower?

Oh, I hope so. I really, really hope so. You can hardly become a full-fledged member of the Laura Corn Grrreat Sex Club without one of these **incredibly sensual** devices! If you don't, well, *get one*. They're not expensive, and *so* worth it; mine cost less than twenty dollars.

You also have stockings and a garter belt, right? You should – let's face it, we're living in the Garter Generation! For over twenty years Playboy and Penthouse have been celebrating these items of **lingerie** above all others, and for two good reasons: every woman looks great in them, and every man is wild about them.

Each one of these ingredients, all by itself, is enough to create a powerful seduction. Imagine the sexual energy you'll conjure up this week when you put them all together... in a small room... with a *very* **aroused man**!

Your invitation was quite specific. Your sweetie is to bring a kitchen chair into the bathroom at precisely the time you choose, and then leave for exactly twenty minutes. What a scene awaits his return: candles cast a **flickering glow** and make the wine glasses sparkle; soft music floats up the hallway. It looks as if every towel in the house has been spread around the floor. Most intriguingly, the shower curtain is *closed*.

"Sit down, lover. I've got something to show you." You slowly pull back the curtain to reveal a sight that will instantly burn its way into his memory; a vision so sexually charged he may never get it out of his head. You're in stockings and garter and bra, of course. (*Huge* bonus points if you do this in **shiny black latex**, available at most upscale adult stores... and even more points for long latex gloves.) You're kneeling in the tub, with the warm, soapy water rising just barely to your bottom. There's something about *wet fabric* that's devastatingly erotic – and this powerful scene is only the beginning of the treat you have in store.

Roll around the tub as you bathe. Play, and splash, and let him watch it all. When you're ready to rinse, drain the tub and grab the handle of your shower massage. Pay *very* special attention to that sweet spot **between your thighs**; take your time, and make sure he sees how much you're enjoying your little water fountain of youth.

Now let him in on the fun. Fold a towel across the edge of the tub and ask him to sit there, feet inside. Kneel between his legs, using another towel for a cushion. Before this moment, your mouth may have given him the **greatest pleasure** he's ever known... but you're about to *double* it. Tease him with your lips, and your hand... *and the water jet*. Aim it every place your mouth isn't. Give him a moment of deep, soft warmth, followed by a moment of stinging spray, and do it again and again. In seconds the constant change and contrast will have him on the toe-curling edge of a thrilling, desperate, please-oh-please-oh-please-don't-stop *orgasm*.

But stop anyway. Tell him to ditch the chair and lay on the towels, *now*. **Straddle him**, grab his ready-to-explode erection, and slip it inside, all the way. Ride that man, as hard as you can; let him feel just how hungry kitty is. Let him know how much you need him. Let him know how much he turns you on.

Let him know he'll be getting a bill for a fancy shower head. (I guarantee he won't complain!)

"In one survey a thousand men were asked what turned them on most: dirty talk, x-rated videos, pornography, female masturbation, sexy lingerie, or "other." Of the men surveyed, 92% said they were most turned on by sexy lingerie. In an interesting footnote, 73% of these men said they relied on stimulation such as this to sustain their interest in a long-term relationship."

-Dr. Patricia Love

Here are your Instructions

Follow them precisely, and they will lead you to an evening of

Extraordinary Sensuality and
Erotic Pleasure

which may or may not include any of the following:

Whips
Poetry
A New Car
Fellatio

Interested? Bring a kitchen chair into the bathroom this

_____ night at precisely _____ o'clock.

Then leave. Take a walk. Do the dishes. But come back to the bathroom

exactly twenty minutes later, no more, no less.

And get ready to have your mind blown.

52 Invitations to Grrreat Sex

n u m b e r 2I

The Unmasking

For Her Eyes Only

"If it is not erotic. It is not interesting."

-Fernando Arrabal

n u m b e r **2 1**

The Unmasking

- 1 robe
- 2 champagne glasses
- Lots of candles

- Lots of tape (Plain old duct tape feels the best. Keep the roll on the bed so he can put more tape on you!)
- 1 close shave

He Brings
Champagne
and other things that go pop

I already know what your first thought is going to be when you read this. *"I can't believe Laura Corn expects me to shave it all off down there!"*

Well, I do. And when you see the result through your lover's eyes, you'll know that it's worth a few days of scratchy stubble. Going bare is an extremely sexy move all by itself, of course – I've interviewed over two thousand men for my research, and the huge majority were just wild over the shaved look – but it's not what this treat is really about.

No, the core of this seduction is something far more erotic. Maybe even just a tiny bit *kinky* – that's what I thought when I saw this in an incredibly **sexy movie** last year. I couldn't believe how aroused I was getting just watching it, and I knew in a heartbeat that I had to try it. So take it from me: *you can do this.* It might sound a little scary at first, but it doesn't hurt. And if your partner is anything like my Jeff, you'll be hearing a **dazed and happy** man talk about this for weeks to come. Here's how it works:

When your lover greets you at the door, nothing seems unusual... at first. The bedroom glows with candles, and you've got glasses waiting for the champagne his invitation requested. You're dressed in a **beautiful** robe, laying back against a big pile of pillows on the bed. Talk, and share a drink, and kiss and laugh, and then stand up next to the bed...

... and unveil yourself. His eyes will pop when he sees that you've got several strips of tape applied to your skin. (I tried masking tape, and clear packing tape, but my favorite is good old-fashioned duct tape. Test it out beforehand, if you like; it comes off easily and doesn't hurt in the least, I promise.) You're striped with big, bold swaths of it, each about a foot long; there's one across your tummy, one over a breast, more on your inner thighs, a few across your buttocks and back, and there's one more – I'll bet you saw this coming! – starting a few inches below your belly-button and **disappearing between** your legs. On this last one you've scrawled a bold message: *Open Last!*

Lean over and kiss him. *"Put your hand on my bottom. Feel that? Now kiss me, and pull the tape awayyy-ahh-ahh-oooOOH, yes, just like that! Now, you get to do all the rest... but you've got to distract me while you're doing it. See, like this; you can take my nipple in your mouth... mmm, that's nice, very good boy... and then grab another strip and oooh WOW yes, oh that really tingles! I think you're getting the idea. Now... surprise me...."*

The feeling is intense; something less than pain but much more than sex. The sheer anticipation can be an excruciating form of pleasure, because you never know where he's going next, or exactly when you'll hear that *swoooooosh* of the tape gently popping each nerve as it pulls from your skin. Like a lover's playful spanking, the slight sting only doubles the rush to ecstasy. As for your mate, well, believe me – this will be fueling his fantasies for the rest of his life. Every twitch of your body, every moan that escapes your lips gives him a **wicked** sense of power, backed by the intimate knowledge that you trust him enough to give him control over your sexuality. By the time he pulls the last bit of wrapping off your special gift – that secret, smooth patch, now revealed as never before – his male ego... and his erection... will be huge.

Fortunately for both of you, this particular present is *one size fits all!*

"If it is not erotic.
It is not interesting."

-Fernando Arrabal

Once Upon A Time

there was a Princess who desperately wished for a Prince to come and

Ravish her, Bare her skin, Caress her breasts, Lift her legs and take her,

bringing her to shocking, unknown heights of Erotic Ecstasy.

In return, she promised to

Grab him, Stroke him, and Submit to his Every Carnal Desire.

You are invited to finally

fulfill her Erotic Fantasy

this _____ *evening at* _____ *o'clock*

in _____

Please bring one (1) bottle of champagne, and

R.S.V.P. by whispering the following message on her answering machine:

"Someday, your Prince will come..."

52 Invitations to Grrreat Sex

n u m b e r 22

Your Mission, Should
You Choose To Accept It $

FOR HIS EYES ONLY

It's hard for me to get used to these changing times. I can remember when the air was clean and the sex was dirty.

-George Burns

n u m b e r **2 2**

Your Mission, Should You Choose To Accept It

i n g r e d i e n t s

- Love notes
- Flowers
- Phone calls
- Kisses
- Backrubs
- Kind words
- Favors
- Snuggles

- Presents
- Squeezes
- Hugs
- Praise
- More kisses
- Ice cream
  And a word of advice: Clean underwear!
  You don't know when she's going to surprise you.

*P*rofessor Corn is about to reveal one of the great *Truths of the Universe: Women don't think like men.* (Quick show of hands – anybody surprised? Anybody?)

Here's what I mean. You love your sweetheart with all your heart and soul, right? You show it every day by busting your butt to provide a nice home and a few luxuries. You fix things. You take care of her car. You take care of *her*. And you're not alone; most guys spend their lives genuinely trying to make their mates happy.

And yet magazines are filled with articles that say men just aren't loving enough. **Your** own lover might appear to be a bit dissatisfied from time to time; just think of the last time she picked a fight for *no apparent freakin' reason at all*. (You thought your woman was the only one who did that? Sit down, kiddo; the Professor has much to teach you.)

The problem is not security. It's desirability. You can be the best breadwinner in the world, but what your lover really needs is to know that you still want her as much as ever. In other words, she wants you to seduce her, just like you did when you first met. It's a never-ending chase. Which, thank God, means job security for me! I'll be happy to spend the rest of my life dreaming up **fabulous seductions** like these.

You can do the same, of course. There are some basic rules you need to follow, and the most important is one I call the Magic Formula: *Anticipation plus Variety equals Total Excitement.*

Simple, huh? But so-o-o-oooo easy to forget. Variety just means surprises and **new experiences** – unfortunately, the very things you run out of when you've been in a relationship for a long time. That's an easy fix, though – hey, you've got an imagination, and this book. (And when you're done with this one, check out my *101 Nights Of Grrreat Sex!*)

Anticipation is more subtle, though – and more powerful. It means finding ways to show your lover you're always thinking of her, and can't wait for the next time you're together. It means teasing her, and letting her know you've got big plans for her. Ultimately, *it's what makes foreplay work.* And this week, you're going to give your mate three straight days of it!

On the surface, this seems like a backward seduction. You're challenging your sweetie to come up with a sensual surprise for *you*. But while she's planning and scheming, you're going to be teasing and flirting. For seventy-two hours, show her how much she thrills you. Let her see that your love – and lust! – burns as brightly as ever: Don't just pop out of bed in the morning – snuggle for fifteen minutes, even if it means setting the alarm early. Call her at work to say *"I miss you."* Leave a love-note taped to the bathroom mirror. Bring flowers! And show her how excited you are about her upcoming treat. *"Oooh, forty-eight hours!"* you'll whisper, as you wrap your arms around her. *"I can hardly wait!"* Before you get out of the car, lean over and kiss her **passionately**. *"Thirty-six hours to go...."* Walk up behind her and rub her shoulders. *"Twenty-two...."* Buy her some new earrings. Kiss her in public.

Unless this is the way you always behave – and ohmigosh, what a lucky lady she is if you do! – then these overtures are going to light a fire in her. She's going to feel that same rush of anticipation that used to flood her heart when she first fell in love. Naturally, she's going to knock herself out to create a treat that will blow you away, and naturally, you're going to express extraordinary delight, no matter what it is. And naturally, after seventy-two hours of foreplay, she's going to be **hot**. She just might do you to death. It would have to be an open-casket service, of course. *"Well, we keep trying to close the lid, but this erection just won't go away...."*

"It's hard for me to get used to these changing times. I can remember when the air was clean and the sex was dirty."

-George Burns

You Are Hereby Challenged

to come up with something — anything — that
We Have Neither Seen Nor Done Before
It must be New. It must be Sex! It must be fun and hot and
wild and perhaps even just a tiny bit Nasty. In short, it must

Turn Me On

Your Reward

will Turn You On. Many times. Over and over. Until you're
glowing, gleaming, gasping for air, aching with pleasure, completely unable to get out of bed. After which I will feed you
Ice Cream.

The Catch

is that you have but 72 Hours to create your treat!
(And no cheating! You can't pull any pages from Laura's book).

R.S.V.P

with a kiss and the phrase...

"The Clock Is Ticking"

52 Invitations to Grrreat Sex

n u m b e r **23**

The Laura Corn Challenge IV

For Her Eyes Only

"To love oneself is the beginning of a life-long romance."

-Oscar Wilde

n u m b e r 23

The Laura Corn Challenge IV

i n g r e d i e n t s

- 1 Fun fearless female!
- 1 Small video camera (Rented, if necessary. I found them for about forty dollars a day.)
- 1 Tripod (Optional, but inexpensive to rent.)

- Pillows (Lots! You can never have too many.)
- Candles (Can't have too many of those, eiher!)
- Music
- Lingerie (As seductive as you can find)

He Brings:
Remote control (for TV)
Toolbox

*I*n each one of my recent books, I've included a seduction called The Laura Corn Challenge. It's always the Big One – an exploration of every man's wildest fantasy; a chance for you to take a deep breath and dive headfirst into your lover's most secret, unspoken desire.

And it's also a chance for you to find strength you didn't know you had. This is a seduction that will weaken his knees almost as much as it fortifies your sexual self-confidence. By the end, you'll finally see yourself through *his* eyes, as a sensual, **powerful**, erotically charged seductress.

Better than that, really – you're going to become a Movie Star!

Rent or borrow a video camera. Me, I'm just lost when it comes to electronic and mechanical toys, so I got the kind with a small built-in TV screen and automatic everything, and I suggest you do the same. Get a tripod, too, so you can just aim it at your bed, press the "record" button, and forget about it.

And then set the stage for your **erotic masterpiece**. Use a few small shaded lamps rather than the glaringly bright ceiling light, or set out a couple of dozen candles. Pile the bed with lots of pillows, and turn on your favorite music. Lock the doors! Put on a sultry, seductive outfit, start the camera, snuggle into the blankets...

And start to play. Inch by inch, **expose your skin**. Run your finger across your bare breast; let the camera see your nipple as it grows taut. Imagine your mate staring, panting, gasping as he watches you pleasure yourself. Imagine his heart racing, his manhood straining for escape, as your hands follow your carnal impulses, tracing a line from hip to thigh to those secret, sensitive folds of flesh. Touch yourself. *Stroke.* Bring yourself to the edge of climax and hover there, waiting, enjoying, moaning until that magic moment when you explode in a rush of hot, wet pleasure.

Every man is a voyeur. Every man harbors a secret wish to watch a woman do what you've just done. And now *your* man is going to have his wish fulfilled in Part Two of the Laura Corn Challenge: the screening.

Your invitation asked him to bring the *remote control* and a *toolbox,* a supply list that will have him scratching his head in wonder and **anticipation** all week. The remote control is obvious, of course – on your special night, with the lights low, the wine poured and the banquet finished, he'll get to start the main feature. Watch his face while he watches your masterpiece. I'll bet you have never seen him more aroused.

He'll be putty in your hands after the show. He'll be **hot** and bothered and begging for the kind of relief only you can grant him. But before you set him loose to fulfill *your* wildest fantasies – and trust me on this, there's *nothing* he won't do for you now – he has one more little job to do:

Open the toolbox. Take out a hammer or a wrench. And destroy the videotape completely.

After all, this isn't the kind of, uh, *coming attraction* you would want anyone else to see!

*"To love oneself is the beginning
of a life-long romance."*

-Oscar Wilde

Your presence is requested at

A Celebration Of Erotic Love
and A Demonstration
Of Its Secret Rituals

to be accompanied by hors d'ouvres and followed by an evening of

Steaming, Passionate Sexual Arousal with Climaxes Aplenty

Your admission will be granted <u>only</u> if you bring:

1) This Invitation

2) The Remote Control to the Television Set

3) A Toolbox

Time:_____

Place:_____

_____

R.S.V.P.

by placing a single red rose on the seat of my car

52 Invitations to Grrreat Sex

n u m b e r 24

Slow Slide

FOR HIS EYES ONLY

"A man is two people, himself and his penis. A man always takes his friend to the party. Of the two, the friend is the nicer, being more able to show his feelings."

-Berly Bainbridge

n u m b e r 24

Slow Slide

i n g r e d i e n t s

- Candles
- Wine
- Warm oil in a bowl

- G-Spot Stimulator, giftwrapped (There are lots of different models, including some that attach to vibrators. Did you know there are nine different techniques for creating an orgasm with the G-spot? They are demonstrated in detail in my *Incredible G-Spot Video* – see the list of my other products in the back of this book)

She Brings:
The G-Spot Stimulator
The wildest imagination

Think with your penis!

Sounds like part of a joke, doesn't it? But guess what? I want you to do exactly that. *Think with your penis.* (And when was the last time you heard a woman make that request?!!)

Specifically, I want you to think about what you're *doing* with your penis. There are a whole lot of wonderful things that can happen between *in* and *out,* and this is the week to focus on them.

Your invitation was accompanied by a beautifully wrapped gift, which came with explicit instructions for your sweetie to bring it, but *not open it.* Set it aside when she greets you at the door. Keep it in plain view so it can keep tickling her curiosity while you light the candles and pour the wine.

Foreplay starts with **kisses and caresses**, but takes a slightly different twist when you introduce her to your penis. Show it to her. Let her watch, completely fascinated, as it starts to swell. She'll be hypnotized by the way it moves, bouncing and dancing as you stroke it. She won't be able to take her eyes off it when you dip your stick into a bowl of warm oil, and she'll be flush with excitement when you slowly draw your slick willie down between her breasts and across her belly. Use it like a paintbrush, trailing massage oil across her thighs, up her arms, all over her face. Gently slap her body with your erection; a light tap on the chin, a tiny smack on her breast.

This is what I mean by *think with your penis.* Use your cock as an **erotic tool**; a finely tuned instrument to turn her on. Tease her. Put it in an inch, no more. Rock back and forth, one slow inch at a time, for five or six minutes at least. Her vagina will be sopping wet and aching for more; when she starts to beg for a push, a solid, **stiff *thrust***, then you've waited long enough. Well, *almost*; let the tension build another minute or two. Finally, let her feel the length of your shaft, and then... pull back. One inch, in and out. Soon she'll be craving deep contact again, and pleading for it. Her little kitty will be howling with hunger by the time you finally start pounding your hips against her bare thighs like a jungle drum.

Explore other ways to use your **erection**. Try pressing the tip of your shaft against the sensitive front wall of her vagina as you glide in – a move that works especially well if you approach her from behind. When you're on top, thrust at an angle, first left, then right, in a move called The Corkscrew. The vagina is an amazing thing – once fully aroused, it can take a *lot* of action. In fact, it can be hard to truly satisfy, but you've got a secret weapon inside that gift box. It's another penis.

Well, not exactly. It's a *G-Spot Stimulator;* a small, slender sort of dildo with a curve, designed to reach that magic spot on the front wall of her vagina. Your sweetie may be afraid to use something so intimate in front of you, but with a little encouragement, she'll start to play. Once it's in...

"I've heard that a lot of women have a fantasy about two men at once," you'll say as you straddle her chest. *"Maybe this is what it would feel like...."*

Oh, I hope you've got a big mirror in the room. What a sight: **Mr. Stiffy disappearing** into her mouth while her hand bounces up and down, tap-tap-tapping the tip of her toy against her humming G-spot. This scene is nothing compared to the very private picture in her head, of course. Please, don't ever ask who she was thinking of. (Or how many!) It's enough to know that of all the men in the fantasy you've just created for her, you're the only one she really loves.

(And the only one who really gets off!)

"*A man is two people, himself and his penis. A man always takes his friend to the party. Of the two, the friend is the nicer, being more able to show his feelings.*"

-Berly Bainbridge

One Red Hot Surprise

is hiding inside this box.

But you must not open it.

It's sexy. It's fun! It will lead us directly to

Sexual Satisfaction

and provide much Erotic

Entertainment

But you must not open it! To repeat:

<u>Do</u> <u>Not</u> <u>Open</u>

until Permission is Granted, which will happen sometime on

_____ evening

beginning at _____ o'clock.

Meet me at _____ .

Bring your imagination. And the box.

R.S.V.P. — If, one evening as I'm reclining on the sofa or bed, you climb on top of me, pull up your shirt and mine, then press those beautiful breasts directly against my bare skin...

... I'll take that as a "yes."

52 Invitations to Grrreat Sex

n u m b e r 25

Pop-Up Sex

FOR HIS EYES ONLY

"The game women play is men."

-Adam Smith

n u m b e r **25**

Pop-Up Sex

i n g r e d i e n t s

• 1 pack of 4x5 index cards   • 1 great big Magic Marker

She Brings:
1 great big Magic Marker
1 great big... oh, wait. You already have that. She just MAKES it big!

*H*ow often are you inspired to have grrreat sex by a television show? (Other than *I Dream Of Jeannie* reruns on Nick At Night, I mean. *"Oooh, yes, Master!"*)

For me, it happened in the middle of Pop-Up Videos. That's the biggest hit on VH-1; the show where they have these clever, outrageous captions popping up in music videos explaining what the drummer was thinking, who the bass player was sleeping with, why the director got fired, stuff like that. Suddenly it hit me. Wouldn't it be cool if I could see Jeff's thoughts pop up over his head while we make love? Wouldn't it be *funny??!*

There's a huge connection between **laughter and sex**, especially for women. You see it in action every week, I'll bet – fairly ordinary guys who never lack for female company because they have the ability to make women laugh. It's a powerful form of foreplay. It always works for me! And it'll work on your lover this week when you follow my recipe for Pop-Up Sex:

Get a stack of 4-by-5 index cards and a big felt-tip pen. Make up your special flash cards in advance, but keep some blank cards handy for last-minute additions. Each day this week you're going to use five or six cards, and I suggest you hide them prior to use by putting them inside a book. When you see an appropriate moment approaching, grab a card or two and get ready to spring them on your **unsuspecting** mate. It'll work something like this –

You spot her in the kitchen. You move into a position so other family members can't see what you're doing. With a sly smile, you hold a card up next to your head; it has an arrow pointing to you and this message: "Has **serious desire** to touch your beautiful bottom." Before she even has time to laugh, you walk over and give her a quick pinch on the tush! Sure, it's silly, but it's also sweet and seductive, and she'll be tickled that you went to all that trouble just to get a laugh and a little bum-squeeze.

Later, more signs, and more laughter. "Willing to take out garbage in return for kisses." "Plagued by foot-fetish **dreams**! Know anyone who wants her feet rubbed?" "Has been imagining you in bra and panties all day."

Keep it up for a few days. Some of these are best if you flash them while other people are just out of sight. "Help! **Uncontrollable** erection developing!" "No one here has any idea how much you turn me on." "Please lift skirt." "Pretty please." "Higher!" "HIGHER!"

By the middle of the week, your invitation will have arrived, asking her to bring a big black Magic Marker to your special rendezvous. She won't have any trouble figuring out the game. As she starts to **undress**: "WOW!!" As you roll around on the bed: "SEX – yes or no?" with little boxes by each answer for her to check off. Hold one with an arrow by your head: "Kiss?" Hold another by your, uh, *other* head: "More kisses?" As your little man becomes the big man, put a caption over it: "Has now taken over all thought processes." Well, *duh!* As if she didn't know that already. In the steamy post-orgasmic afterglow, put this one over your head: "Thinks you are greatest lover in history of world." And this over your deflated manhood: "Elvis has left the building!"

Later, after sharing a snuggle and some laughs, pay her a final compliment. Hand her the Magic Marker, and pop one last card over tired old Mr. Happy. "You're the best. Can I have your autograph?" Let her sign her name to her handiwork. And if there's not enough room for her whole signature, well, wait a few minutes.

Something's sure to Pop Up!

"The game women play is men."

-Adam Smith

You are invited to experience the new and

highly entertaining game of

Pop-Up Sex

Where the only rules are... well, okay, there are no rules. I'm

going to make them up as we go along. But you are

guaranteed to have:

Foreplay, as much as you wish

Sex,

Laughs,

More Sex

And at least One awesome

Climax

In return, you are required to bring

A Large Black Felt-Tip Pen

An Open Attitude and

Your Beautiful Smile

to the bedroom door

Time: _____

Date: _____

Attire: Casual, and easy to remove.

52 Invitations to Grrreat Sex

n u m b e r 26

She's A Spinner $

For Her Eyes Only

"How are men just like tiles? Because if you lay them right the first time, you can walk all over them the rest of your life."

-Anonymous

n u m b e r **26**

She's A Spinner

i n g r e d i e n t s

- 1 Kama Sutra book (Anne Hooper's is the best)
- 10 pieces of tracing paper
- 10 places to surprise him with your art
- 5 positions for you to initiate

- 5 positions for him to initiate
- 100 bonus points and a gold medal if you can get through all 10!
- 1 pencil

He Brings:
Whatever you like to celebrate with (write it on the invitation)
3 pulled muscles!

How many sexual positions do you know?

I thought I knew a lot – after all, I write books about lovemaking! – until the day I stumbled across the Kama Sutra, the granddaddy of all sex manuals. Ohmigosh! Early Indian civilization was *not* the way they taught us in school!

The original ancient manuscripts have been reinterpreted by a number of contemporary authors; the version I recommend is by Anne Hooper. Go buy it. It will enrich your **love life** for years to come. And you'll need it to carry off this week's seduction, which isn't really about how many sexual positions you know. It's about how many you *initiate.*

Men have a word for a woman who is, above all, enthusiastic about sex. *"She's a spinner,"* they say, with a smile on their faces. I love the image that conjures up! Well, this week you're going to show your mate that *you* are a spinner. You're going to spin from position to position; you're going to spin on him, and with him. Most of all, you're going to spin his head around with a display of more sheer excitement and enthusiasm than he's ever seen in bed. Even **your teases** will spin his eyeballs. Here's what I mean:

Go through the Kama Sutra book and pick out some intriguing illustrations. Find five for him, and five for you, that you've never done before. Now copy them from the book. Xerox? If you must, but I suggest a much more interesting and attractive method: *trace them.* Uh-huh, just like you did as a schoolkid. Get some tracing paper and sketch outlines of these highly **erotic positions**. Fold the first one up and put it in the envelope with your invitation.

Think that'll get his attention? As the days go buy, leave more of them where he'll find them. Put one on the seat of his car with a note scribbled on it: *"Study this!"* Tape one to the bathroom mirror: *"You will be tested."* Leave one in his jacket pocket: *"Can't wait to see what you do with this!"*

On the evening of your seduction, leave the book out in plain sight. Here's another secret the ancients discovered – looking through **erotic pictures** is a terrific form of foreplay! There's *The Rainbow Arch... The Tail Of The Ostrich... Love's Fusion... The Placid Embrace.* Pick out the ones you want to try – limber up first! – and dive right in. Here's one of my favorites:

Have him lay on his back and pull his knees up to his chest. Straddle him, grab his ankles, and lower yourself onto his **dancing erection**. Now you have complete control; you can do whatever you want with throbbing penis. Instead of the traditional in-and-out movement, *bend it.* Rock your hips as you slide down the length of his slick shaft; pull it back and forth. Mr. Friendly loves a real workout, and can take a lot more abuse than you think, so grind, and twist, and push that sexy thing around in circles. Don't be afraid to be rough; his thighs and hips are the strongest part of him, and can easily take your full weight. (Notice that this is the exact reverse of a common male-superior position, and that he's getting it the way most women do. He may be indulging in some *very* nasty fantasies about now!)

I love the title of this position. It's called *The Race Of The Member,* and it's based on – have you figured it out already? – horseback riding! Yep, you're in the saddle, bouncing and **squeezing and riding** like you're about to win the Triple Crown, only better. Because in this race, it doesn't matter who comes in first and who comes in second.

Just as long as everybody comes!

"How are men just like tiles? Because if you lay them right the first time, you can walk all over them the rest of your life."

-Anonymous

Your Lover Presents:

The Art Of Desire

A lesson in the finer points of Supreme Sexual Pleasure, as described by the

ancient and revered courtesans and hedonists of The Sub-Continent.

You are strongly urged to spend the week Limbering Up and Stretching Your

Muscles as you will find the quality of the Many Orgasms you encounter to

be greatly diminished by any strains or sprains. Among the muscles on which

you should most concentrate are:

The Legs
The Back
The Tongue

It is also recommended that you bring

_____

_____

in order to celebrate your graduation from this class in Sensual Seduction.

Place: _____

Date: _____

Time: _____

R.S.V.P. – write a note of acceptance on the enclosed drawing

and leave it where I will find it.

52 Invitations to Grrreat Sex

n u m b e r **27**

The Diddler $

FOR HIS EYES ONLY

> *"The reason so many women fake orgasms*
> *is that so many men fake foreplay"*
>
> -Anonymous

n u m b e r 27

The Diddler

i n g r e d i e n t s

• One candle
• 1 brand new and very sexy pair of panties
• Scented wrapping paper (or a gift box)

• 1 hot movie (My pick? The sensual and almost unbe-lievably beautiful Kama Sutra. Subtitled, but there's not a lot of talking going on! I still get wet watching Body Heat. In the adult genre, anything by Andrew Blake.)

She Brings:
The panties

First base, second base, third base. Mashing. Scamming. When I was in high school we called it heavy petting. As long as there have been virgins, there have been words to describe the act of *not quite* going all the way.

Go ahead, take a moment to think about your first sexual contact – the first time you slid a hand under a bra or between a pair of hot, **trembling thighs**. Remember the exquisite torture of being allowed – *finally!* – to touch her panties, with all that warm girl skin just a thin layer of fabric away. Brings a smile to your face, doesn't it? Believe me, it's the same for women. Thrilling, exciting, scary, intensely erotic (and of course, ultimately frustrating!), those old hands-everywhere makeout sessions are now treasured memories.

You're going to recreate that fabulous feeling for your lover this week, with a very grown-up twist. And since the most important ingredient in this **seduction** is the underwear, you might as well get the best. Drop by Victoria's Secret and pick out a pair in satin, cotton or lace. Have them wrapped in soft, scented paper, and then find some place to hide them.

Have some fun with this part! I've left a blank spot at the bottom of your invitation so you can write out a clue. Are they hidden in the glove box of your car? Then "Vrooom!" is a pretty good hint. In your stereo cabinet? How about "Crank it up!" for rockers, or maybe "dit-dit-dit-DAH!" for Beethoven buffs. "Imelda Marcos" would lead her to a shoebox, don't you think?

She'll grin when she reads the note attached to the panties: *"Please meet me Friday night at eight in the living room. Wear these under a loose skirt. And no matter what happens – <u>you must not take them off!</u>"*

At the appointed hour, take her into your arms and whisper into her ear – *"Are you wearing your new panties? Yes? Show me...."* Put a sexy movie in the VCR and sprawl on the sofa. (Kids in the house? Then make your bedroom into a mini-theater.) The next couple of hours are one long tease, just as if you were back in high school. **Kiss her neck**. Brush your hand across her blouse. Slowly, *slowly* go for third base, squeezing your fingertips against the shiny, soft cage holding her hungry kitty at bay. She wants more – the dampness soaking through the fabric proves she wants more – but don't take the panties off.

Instead, use them to stimulate her. Slide the slick material across her lips; press it against her aching clit. Kneel before her open thighs and rub your face against her vulva. Let her feel your hot, moist breath through the cloth, and then **nibble**, chewing the smooth fabric itself ever so gently. Pour warm massage oil onto your hand and let it trickle like honey over her panties; work it through the fabric and into her tingling lips with your fingers. Go ahead and pleasure yourself, too; pull that big, stiff rod out of your trousers. By the time the movie is close to the end, you've been going at this for *hours,* and now you're both throbbing, aching, screaming for sexual release. Ah, but this date doesn't have to end. This time you get to go all the way....

Still, you've got to keep those panties on! Slip a finger under the edge and pull them aside; put the tip of your erection against that hot, wet desperate-to-be-filled hole **and *push***. You'll feel the elastic rubbing against your penis with every thrust; she'll feel it taut against her clitoris; you'll both feel like a couple of horny teenagers trying to get off without getting caught.

Oh, wait a second. *I* caught you, didn't I? Okay, you two, you're grounded for the whole weekend. Now go to your rooms... I mean, room... and don't come out until I say so....

"*The reason so many women fake orgasms is that so many men fake foreplay*"

-Anonymous

At the Bottom of this Invitation is

A Clue

to the location of

A Very Special and very Sexy Gift

You must Find the Gift
and Follow the
Attached Instructions.

Successful Completion of this Treasure Hunt

will be Rewarded with

A Weekend Full of Foreplay, Surprises,

and Orgasms of all Shapes and Sizes

Here is your special Clue:

_____

52 Invitations to Grrreat Sex

n u m b e r 28

Heads or Tails

FOR HIS EYES ONLY

"The greatest discovery of the twentieth century is that women like it too."

-George Burns

n u m b e r **2 8**

Heads or Tails

- 1 dresser or desk
- 1 pillow
- *Anything* that will make her shiver

She Brings:
Lingerie of lace
Coins of nickel
Nerves of steel

*H*ow many erogenous zones do you have? Other than *that* one, I mean! (Although I have to admit, that's one heckuva great zone. My very favorite on a guy.)

Besides the obvious places, the human body can find pleasure in dozens of spots. With the right attention, almost any inch of skin can be **tantalized, tickled, and turned on**. This week, you're going to devote an evening to finding as many ways as possible to make your lover shiver with delight.

She's going to show up at the bedroom door wondering why your invitation asked her to bring <u>two shiny nickels</u>. *"Oh, it's the price of admission to my new game,"* you can tell her as you take the coins. *"It requires a bit of skin, though...."* Help her undress, and once she's down to her panties and bra (or better yet, a lacy, sexy teddy), put a pillow on the dresser and invite her to bend over it. She should be quite comfortable like this: legs straight and slightly apart, arms and head resting on the pillow. *"Here's the game. I'm going to put one nickel on the back of each wrist. Let's see how long you can keep them there!"* Ah, now's that's a challenge! She has to stay perfectly still – while you **use every erotic trick** you know to make her tremble. Count out loud every time a coin falls and has to be put back in place.

Now touch her. Touch her everywhere, and always in at least two places at once. Sometimes you'll use the *Hover Massage,* a technique where your hand grazes only her fine body hair, sending tingles of static **electricity** into her skin. Try this:

- Caress her face with your fingertips while your lips graze her ears.
- Kiss her neck while reaching around front to tweak her nipples.
- Slip one hand between her legs while massaging her neck with the other.
- Hover over the front of her thighs while kissing her bottom.
- Press your fingers against her clit, then run your tongue in one slow swipe from the base of her spine all the way up to her neck. If that doesn't turn her knees to jelly, she's dead!

After a while, move her to the bed, face up, arms at her sides. Keep counting every time she trembles enough to knock a coin off her wrists, while you:

- Hover up her legs while sucking her toes.
- Gently pinch a nipple while running your tongue from hip to hip.
- Stretch her nipple taut. This makes it stiff and immobile and so, so sensitive; she'll gasp when you lick it.

Here's a technique that may bounce those nickels off your ceiling! Gently press your palm into her *Mons Veneris,* the little bulge where her pubic hair grows. Pull her flesh in small, slow circles with your palm. As the skin of her mons slides around, it stretches all those lovely, sexually charged nerves in her lips and clitoris. After half a minute, stop your **tender tugging**, lift your fingers, and tap then against her vaginal lips. Tap... tap... tap... lightly, once or twice per second.

Ten taps, then rub your palm in ten circles. Tap again, then massage with your hand. Repeat until she melts. I call it *Palmreading, Laura Corn style,* because it's easy to read her reaction to your palm: she'll be gasping and moaning and visibly struggling to keep those nickels in place.

Game over. How many times has she dropped them? *"Oooh, that's the number of favors you're going to do for me,"* you whisper as you **climb on top of her**, filling her soaked and aching, desperate-for-climax little hole. *"One coin, one sexual favor. You're in debt right now, but don't worry. You get to knock the nickels off <u>me</u> next time...."*

Until then, you've got some decisions to make. You won, so what are you going to claim for your reward? Maybe you should toss a coin:

Head? Or tail?

"*The greatest discovery of the twentieth century is that women like it too.*"

-George Burns

The Nickel Game

I have a new game that I'd like you to play.
You're going to like it a lot!
It starts with sex
And ends with sex
The sex in the middle is hot.

Remember, it's not if you win or lose,
What matters is taking a shot.
If you want to play
Bring some nice lingerie
And two nickels to throw in the pot.

So what prize should go to the winner?
The nickels might help us to choose
One side is head
The other is tail
In this game there's no way to lose!

Date:_____

Time:_____

Place:_____

You must bring:
a bit of sexy underwear and
Two Shiny Nickels

(Be prepared to flip!)

R.S.V.P.
If you're going to come, you'll need some change.
Feel free to rummage through the front pocket of my pants…
…while I'm wearing them. And take your time.

52 Invitations to Grrreat Sex

n u m b e r 29

Heels & Squeals

For Her Eyes Only

"The heels push my ass, real high, and make me taller.
They give me an advantage over my client. I put them on and
get a rush of power, knowing I could waste any man I choose to.
I am not a violent woman, not really, but in stilettos I become
real aggressive. High spiked heels bring out the tigress in me."

-Manhattan Call Girl

n u m b e r 29

Heels & Squeals

i n g r e d i e n t s

- 1 fabulous outfit (no panties!)
- 2 high heels (the kind that scream, "Do me now!")
- 2 chairs
- 1 hot adult film (For classics, you can't beat "The Devil In Miss Jones." The current master of quality couples-oriented erotica is Andrew Blake. Lush sets, gorgeous people, convincing chemistry; he makes erotica with women in mind. Look for his "Wet" or "Delirious.")
- A whole lot of confidence

He Brings
1 new pair of boxers
Anything you write on those blank lines – food, wine, a marching band, whatever you desire.
1 out-of-control penis
1 easily-controlled brain

*Q*uick: what's the first thing that pops into your head when I say the name Sharon Stone?

I'll bet it's that scene in Basic Instinct. *Wow!* She gave the world the most famous quarter-second in movie history when she uncrossed her legs and showed that they were **bare** all the way to the top... and then some.

That brief flash up her skirt turned her into a screen legend. (And a wealthy one; her salary went from one million to ten million dollars after that film.) Men the world over **melted** in their seats. Two men left their wives for her! One millionaire after another tried to win her favor. *But it could have happened to someone else.*

That's right. Lots of actresses turned down that role. Sharon's laughing all the way to the bank because she had one thing they didn't: *sexual confidence*. She knew that we women have the power to stop men dead in their tracks. We can make them do what we want. And we can do it with nothing more than Sharon used in that classic scene – a wicked smile, a pair of strappy high heels, and a skirt with nothing underneath.

That's your uniform for this week's seduction. Oh, you should dress it up a bit; add a camisole, blouse, a nice jacket, your best jewelry. But **underneath, there's nothing** between you and fresh air. When your lover arrives, he'll be knocked out by your sharp look, and you should keep him on the defensive by immediately taking control. *"Sit down, Sweetie, and let me explain the rules...."*

As you speak, he'll notice that there's a movie playing on the teevee, and... holy cow, it's hot! It's an adult film, and he can't take his eyes off it – until you sit down across from him and make like Ms. Stone. *"We're going to watch this movie together. And you're going to behave yourself."* **Flash him**. Pull a foot onto the chair so he sees what's *not* under your skirt. *"You can't do anything I'm not doing. You can't touch me unless I say so. You can't touch yourself without permission."* Smile your best aren't-you-lucky-to-be-with-me smile, and kneel before him. *"Now, weren't you supposed to be wearing a brand new pair of boxers? Let me see...."*

Pull off his shoes, socks and pants. Then remove your jacket, unbutton your blouse... and stop. Sit back and enjoy the movie. Feel the tension throbbing through the room. It's almost unbearable; you're watching the steamiest erotic action – *but you can't touch each other*. The sexual anticipation crackles between your chairs like **electricity**.

While the show heats up the screen, you can heat up your mate. Play with your sexy shoes. Let him see straight up your thighs. After a while, reach down and lazily draw your fingers through your moist and swelling folds.

Your man will be sizzling. *"Mmm, honey, it's getting so warm in here,"* you moan as you shrug off your blouse. Make him strip to his shorts. *"Go ahead. Touch yourself. I want to see you make it hard."* Ohhh, yeah; he's ready to do anything you say right now. Anything at all.

And he'll never forget this scene as long as he lives: you, in jewels and a lacy bra, skirt hiked up, fingers dancing around your glistening clit, with those fabulous high heels bouncing at the end of your legs, draped over the arms of the chair. He is yours to command. **He salutes you** with his cock.

"Oh, that's nice. Such a big, hard penis. I want it." It's yours. *"Come here and show me what you can do with it."* He's there. The sex that follows will be hot, wild, animalistic; he no longer controls the beast you've been **teasing**. Furniture will be moved tonight. And even when it's over, the fun doesn't have to end:

Rewind. Play.

"The heels push my ass, real high, and make me taller. They give me an advantage over my client. I put them on and get a rush of power, knowing I could waste any man I choose to. I am not a violent woman, not really, but in stilettos I become real aggressive. High spiked heels bring out the tigress in me."

-Manhattan Call Girl

Double Feature

Two great shows for the price of one!
One is sultry and steamy and so very sexy,
The other is hotter – it is sex.

Bring_____

and_____

and wear a brand new pair of boxers.

It's going to be a Blockbuster night....

*Date:*_____

*Time:*_____

*Place:*_____

R.S.V.P. any day this week by doing your best Siskel & Ebert impression...

... "Three thumbs up!"

52 Invitations to Grrreat Sex

n u m b e r 30

The Right Tool For The Job $

FOR HIS EYES ONLY

"Nobody will ever win the battle of the sexes.
There's too much fraternizing with the enemy."

-Henry Kissinger

n u m b e r 3O

The Right Tool For The Job

(continued)
Now about those blank lines in the invitation –

Too soft:	**Just right:**	**WAY off base:**
"adore you"	"crave your body"	"fantasize about sheep?"
"love"	"simmering lust"	"back hair growing"
"kiss"	"make love"	"get drunk"
"heart"	"nipples, even my earlobes"	"sphincter"
"burst"	"come"	"loosen uncontrollably"
"mere presence"	"mouth"	"mother"
"want to be a better man"	"so hard I could cut diamonds"	"have nightmares"
"a passionate kiss"	"night of total sexual indulgence"	"brand new Lexus"
"anytime"	"right then, right there"	"just as soon as we pay
"mentally"	"by my mind"	off your freaking
"physically"	"body the erect part"	credit card bills"
		"by lap-dancing at a
		Navy base"
		"giving all your tips to me"

i n g r e d i e n t s

- Wine, candles, music
- Notebook, with one question written on each page

She Brings:
A pen
More words than you would believe possible
A growing sexual obsession with *your* words – and you!

"12 Questions To Ask Before You Stay The Night" – "The Good Girl, Bad Girl Quiz!" – "Is He The One For You? Take This Quiz And Find Out!"

Have you seen those women's magazines in the supermarkets and bookstores? Every one of them has some screaming headline asking readers to dive inside and take a quiz – "The Sex Quiz That Will Change Your Life!"

They do it because it *works*, of course. Women adore quizzes. John Gray explains why in his multi-zillion-selling book *Men Are From Mars, Women Are From Venus*. Women love words, he says. Words sustain friendships and heal wounds and – make a note here – **words turn women on**. More than anything else, women love being listened to. That's the power behind those quizzes; it's important for a woman to explain how she feels about a topic... even if she's the only one listening.

So give her what she wants. Yep, I mean a quiz, with your undivided attention. Buy a notebook or journal at any stationery store, pick ten or fifteen of the following questions – feel free to make up your own, of course – then write a single one at the top of each page:

- Is there anything I could do, in or out of the bedroom, to make you happier?
- What's your favorite type of kiss? Your favorite **flavor of lips**?
- What kind of foreplay can you never get enough of?
- What smells are sexy to you?

Your date begins with wine, candles, and soft music. Climb into bed with her and pull out your journal. Drink in every word of her replies....

- What is bad sex?
- What do you love most about having sex?
- What do you get from **oral sex** that you don't get from intercourse?

Write down her answer underneath each question. She'll be more than flattered; this is a true **aphrodisiac** for a woman. It won't be long before you see a fire burning in her eyes.

- What is the one sexual fantasy you think about most?
- What is the difference between sex and making love?
- How many times do you like to be brought to the brink of orgasm before it actually happens?
- How many different kinds of orgasm do you have? Which ones are stronger?
- What words could I whisper in your ear right before you **climax** in order to intensify your orgasm?

With every question, she'll feel more connected to you. With every answer you write down, her sexual temperature will rise. Finally, close the book and kiss her, hard and passionately. Be prepared for an intense reaction; the sex that follows may be fast and furious...

... *and virtually unlimited*. That's because of another feminine quality: we're curious. She's going to want to know what you wrote... and you won't tell her! In fact, you're going to *hide the journal*. Every so often she'll look up see you reading through it (or pretending to!), and no matter how busy she might be, she's going to start thinking about sex. She'll begin to **obsess** about it. She'll want it, and before you know it she'll be dragging you to the closest private room to push you down, strip you bare and jump all over you. And that's because of another quality in women: we're perpetually, unstoppably, **unbelievably horny**.

Oh, wait. That's *you* guys! Whatever.

"*Nobody will ever win the battle of the sexes. There's too much fraternizing with the enemy.*"

-Henry Kissinger

Questions:

Did you know that I _____?

Can you feel my _____ when you walk into the room?

Whenever we _____ I feel as if

my _____ could _____.

Your _____

makes me _____.

I have more questions for you —
and if you have the right answers,

You will win a _____,

delivered _____.

Bring One Fine Pen

and get ready to be tested _____

and _____

Date: _____

Time: _____

Place: _____

R.S.V.P. by picking a time and place where no one else can

see what you're doing, even if there's a crowd nearby...

... and flashing me.

52 Invitations to Grrreat Sex

n u m b e r 3I

Brinksmanship

FOR HIS EYES ONLY

*"Life is a banquet and most damned fools
are starving to death."*

-Auntie Mame

n u m b e r 3 1

Brinksmanship

- (Note: Put anything you like in the blanks on the invitation. Have fun!)
- 1 kitchen timer (A 3-minute egg timer is best)
- 1 note with your secret desire
- 1 envelope to seal it in
- All the self-control you can muster

She Brings:
Her secret desire, sealed in an envelope
The upper hand (Hey! She's a woman!)

"Anything you can do, I can do better; I can do anything better than you!" Okay, I admit it. As a kid, I was a sore loser. (Sidenote to my brothers: this admission is not an apology!! And I can *still* beat you both at Monopoly!)

I can't resist a good challenge, and I like to win. I'll bet you feel the same, right? Well, here's a game that has it all – high stakes, simple rules, a level playing field... and it's so much fun that even *losing* will leave you with **a smile**!

It's the ultimate test of your bedroom skills, and it starts when your lover meets you in the bedroom carrying a sealed envelope. You've got one, too; they both contain the stakes of the game... but neither of you knows what the other is betting. If she wins, you'll open her envelope and do what she's written. And if you win – ohhh, *mama* – she'll have to grant you your **secret wish**.

Don't get carried away. You can't ask her for three knob jobs a day for the rest of your life. And she can't demand a ski condo in Vail. The bet can only be for something you have the *power to deliver in three days,* which pretty well rules out that new Lexus. But will you end up washing dishes for a few days? Will she have to perform a striptease for you? Let the games begin!

"I'll bet I can make you come faster than you can make me come," you'll explain. Ho ho! I doubt that very much, she's thinking. *"I'm going to set this timer for three minutes. I'll do everything I can to turn you on until the timer goes off. Then we reset it... and it's your turn to do me. Three minutes later, I'll try to bring you to an **orgasm**, and three minutes after that, you do the same."*

"Back and forth we go, and when one of us has a climax, the other wins. Got it? Let's go!"

Make an elaborate gesture out of cranking the timer and setting it on the nightstand. Then grab her, toss her on the bed, and get busy. Tug her jeans off; open her blouse. Kiss and rub and touch and... *r-r-rrring!* There's the timer. Reset, and enjoy her handiwork. No sense resisting, at least until you're on the brink. *R-r-rrring!* Your turn again. She's **naked now**, and ready for some serious attention; cup the cheeks of her butt in your hands and pull her hips to your mouth. Mmm... lick and flicker and nibble and... *r-r-rrring!*

Let her tease you. Let her suck you. Let her press those pretty titties into your face. She's good, no doubt, but you only have to hold out for three minutes and then... *r-r-rrring!* Turn her on her tummy, slip your hand between her cheeks; bite the back of her neck while diddling her with your fingers. Snake your thumb into her hot little hole and **tickle her** G-spot while your fingers dance on her clitoris. *R-r-rrring!*

Each round brings you closer to the brink. Each tick of the timer puts her closer to heaven. Each of you will be attempting to get as close to the edge as possible without going over, while pushing the other as hard as you can. No one wants to give up bragging rights as Best Lover but, ohmigod, how long can you stand this level of intense stimulation? I see three potential outcomes:

1. One of you finally says *to hell with it, I don't care if I lose* and goes over the top. 2. One of you really *does* **lose control**, and explodes in the biggest, loudest sheet-drenching climax of your life. Or 3. You grab a big book, smash that timer into bits, and screw like bunnies the rest of the night.

I'm not going to tell you what happened the night I challenged Jeff to this contest. Let's just say that I ended up with a really nice new *r-r-rrring!*

*"Life is a banquet
and most damned fools are
starving to death."*

-Auntie Mame

Wanna bet?

What would you like to win from me?

Chores? Time?_____?

How about _____?

Maybe _____? Or _____?

Perhaps your favorite form of Erogenous Attention?

I will grant you anything that's in my power to deliver

Within 3 Days...

Only If You Win My New Bedroom Game.

It's the ultimate test of erotic skills; so much fun that even losing isn't bad. Not that I will ever know, because
I Am Going To Win!

Write down your secret desire...
Seal it in an envelope... And bring it with you.
(Guess what — I'm going to do the same!)

Date:_____

Time:_____

Arena:_____

For this kind of contest, even the warmup exercises are fun!

R.S.V.P.

If you accept my challenge and will attend the Bedroom

Olympics, simply play _____ on the stereo

one evening this week. And dance to it.

52 Invitations to Grrreat Sex

n u m b e r 32

Sneak Attack $ $

For Her Eyes Only

"One of my role models; Xena, the Warrior Princess."

-Madeleine Albright

n u m b e r **32**

Sneak Attack

i n g r e d i e n t s

- 1 Room with movies-on-demand (Or a VCR. Call around; even mid- and low-priced hotels offer this service these days)
- 1 hot film
- Candles

He Brings
A change of undies
A glowing review: <u>three</u> thumbs up!

*A*re you sitting down? Because I've got some shocking news: *Men sometimes lie to get sex!*

Oh. You don't look surprised. Maybe you've heard this before, then. Well, it's sad but true; sex is such a powerful drive that some men – none you and I know *personally*, of course – will make stuff up in order to get us into bed with them.

We women, on the other hand, never need to lie. Uh-uh. We're more **creative** than that. Makeup? Just an enhancement! Wonder bras? Well, they *start* with the truth. "Have there ever been any other men besides me, dear?" *Uhhhh....*

Well, okay, a little fib can be a good thing. But for this seduction, you're going to trick your lover with the absolute truth. You *are* going to a movie, just like your invitation said. But not exactly the way he had in mind.

These days there are a lot of hotels that offer *movies on demand* – that is, they have a special system which allows you to choose from a menu of movies, order one from the **privacy** of your room, and have it start playing on your television screen right away. Some of these movies are hot adult films. And I'll bet you can see where this seduction is going....

Your lover will be excited before your date even starts. A movie is fun... but what was that in the invitation about bringing an extra pair of underwear?? Sounds like sex might be on the agenda! And so it is... much sooner than he has **imagined**.

On your way to the "theater," flirt with your man. Tease him, and touch him; grab his hand and put it high on your thigh while he drives. In just a few minutes he'll start to regret the movie idea; getting bare with his baby sounds so much better. Watch his face when you tell him to slow down... and turn into the parking lot of a hotel. *He's curious... puzzled... hmm, maybe he's starting to get it... yes, there's a little light bulb going off in his head now....*

"Pull up over there, by that room. Wait here five minutes," you'll say as you **hand him a key**, *"and then come inside."*

Yes!! He was right! There *is* no movie; you were planning something all along, and now – *whooo-eeee boy!* – he's gonna get some!

You were at the hotel earlier, reserving the room, getting keys, placing candles. Just one thing left to do: start the movie. By the time he walks in he'll see you on the bed, shoes off, blouse unbuttoned, and on the tube there are **beautiful naked people** rolling around. Gee, it seems that there is going to be a movie after all... and what a picture! *"Come here,"* you whisper. *"It's showtime."*

Grab him and pull him on the bed. Strip him as fast as you can. As often as possible, keep one hand wrapped around his throbbing erection. Even when you stop to catch your breath and watch the movie, you should be stroking and tugging and squeezing his rigid shaft. Follow the action in the movie: Take him in your mouth, climb right up on his face, **spread your legs** wide and beg him to fill you, just like the actors on the screen.

There's a freedom that comes with a quickie in hotel room – you don't have to clean up, no one can bother you – and a huge thrill that comes from watching others doing what you're doing. But the biggest rush is the suddenness of it all, the intense, hot fast-and-furious nature of your **sexual sneak attack**. You might have planned it all, but for your lover, this is the greatest quickie of his life.

And hey – the room's paid for. No reason why you can't turn this into a double-feature!

"One of my role models;
Xena, the Warrior Princess."

-Madeleine Albright

Lights... Camera... A-a-aanndd

(you are going to get so much)

Action!

I would like to treat you to Dinner and a Movie...
(And since you are likely to <u>Be</u> the Dinner
I suggest you bring along an extra pair of underwear!)
Don't be late. You won't want to miss my coming attractions.

*Date:*_____

*Time:*_____

Pick me up at home... and be ready for an
Oscar®-winning performance

If you can't go, well, too bad.
I'll guess I'll have to start the show without you.

If you <u>can</u> make it, here's how to R.S.V.P. –

Chase me around the house. Catch me. (If you can!)

Hold me down and tug off my panties. (If you can!)

Spank my bare bottom until I squeal, then

Kiss it until it feels better. (You <u>can</u>!!)

52 Invitations to Grrreat Sex

n u m b e r 33

My Penis Made Me Do It!

FOR HIS EYES ONLY

"To succeed with the opposite sex, tell her you're impotent. She can't wait to disprove it."

-Cary Grant

number **33**

My Penis Made Me Do It!

i n g r e d i e n t s

- 1 very small gift (I suggest a chocolate truffle in a box)
- 1 roll of plastic wrap
- Boxer shorts

- Bathrobe
  (If your budget allows, go for the gold: hang a bit of jewelry down there with your jewels. For a very impressive tease, put your gift inside a locked box on the dresser. Let her see it for a few days before challenging her to find the key!)

She Brings:
Warm-up suit
Birthday suit!

Okay, I'm going to throw a formula at you, but don't panic. It's not exactly higher math. (My Jeff likes to say it's *lower* math. Arithmetic from below the belt!) I call it the Erotic Equation, and it explains why sex is sometimes so much hotter than other times.

Attraction + Obstacles = Excitement

Simple, huh? The sex that's difficult to achieve is the sweetest of all. Think of the times you were fooling around while your girlfriend's parents were nearby, or you were almost caught. Have you ever been separated from your lover for days or weeks, and then found your reunion turning into a marathon sexfest? Girls play hard-to-get because their mothers teach them to, but *women* do it because it makes the "getting" so much more intense. You'll find the **Erotic Equation** all through this book, built right into seductions like this one:

Women adore surprises, and we love getting gifts, both of which you promised her in your invitation. She'll be bouncing on her toes when she meets your for your date, excited about seeing what you have for her. *"Well, it's hidden,"* you say with a sly smile. *"It's somewhere in this room... but you have to find it."*

Oooh! What fun! No woman can resist a **treasure hunt**. She'll check the closet, the drawers, the furniture. Soon you'll ask her if she'd like a hint. *"You're getting colder... colder...."* She'll open things, and poke through things, and peer under piles of things. *"Hmm, now you're warmer. Getting warmer...."*

It dawns on her that she's warmer when she's nearer to you. She heads in your direction. *"Oh, my, you're getting much warmer. Starting to get hot...."* She reaches for your bathrobe, but before she can get a grip – you turn and run!

Lead her on a merry chase through the house. *"Oh, you're so cold; you're an ice cube now!"* **you tease** as you pull away. When she catches up: *"Warmerwarmerwarmerwarmer...."* Stay just a bit ahead of her until you've circled back to the bedroom and she tugs your robe open. All she sees underneath is boxer shorts, so she grabs for them. *"Hotter! Hotter!"* Don't make it easy, put up enough fight to make her work for her victory.

Down go the shorts. Up go her eyebrows! Under your undies is several layers of Saran Wrap™, all around your **hips** and wrapped extensively around your penis. *"Much hotter! You're burning!"*

Through the plastic she sees something besides flesh. It looks like it might be a small box, dangling just below your own wrapped package. Now break away and run again – *"Cooling off! Cooler! Getting cold!"* She'll catch you again, of course, and start to **tear off the plastic** sheets. And sure enough, it's a tiny, beautifully wrapped gift, tied to your bad boy with a ribbon. *"Okay, okay... get it off, and it's yours."*

Oh, she'll get it off, all right. The gift, I mean – though the process of unwrapping and pulling and untying and tugging may be enough to get *you* off! Her face will be flush from your chase, her eyes will be **sparkling with anticipation**, and the sheer silly playfulness of your game will leave her giggling and happy. It almost doesn't matter what's inside the tiny box, but I think a *single chocolate truffle* would be perfect. It's so yummy, and full of all those luscious brain-tickling love chemicals. And that thick, rich creamy center just screams, *"Spread me on nipples! Smear me across lips! Dab me on penises! Lick me lick me lick me!!"*

"To succeed with the opposite sex, tell her you're impotent. She can't wait to disprove it."

-Cary Grant

Here's a lesson they were afraid to teach you in school...

The Erotic Equation:
Attraction + Obstacles = Excitement

The Obstacle Course is waiting.

So is your Prize, if you make your way through.

Pass, and you're guaranteed a

Great Big Standing "O" at the Awards Ceremony

Plus the Sensual Surprises reserved only for Honor Students

(Fail, and Teacher will drill you after class!)

Location: _____

Date: _____

The bell rings at: _____

R.S.V.P.

A simple "yes" will do. Written in lipstick.

On my rearview mirror.

52 Invitations to Grrreat Sex

n u m b e r 34

Three Way Girl $ $

FOR HIS EYES ONLY

"The only known aphrodisiac is variety"

-Marc Connolly

n u m b e r 34

Three Way Girl

- 1 Small butt plug (And if you don't use one, put a vibrator on her vulva, a dildo inside, and your tongue on her clit. And presto: she's still a three-way girl!)
- 1 Dildo (Again, not the biggest one in the store! Go to your favorite adult boutique, or call Good Vibrations™: 1-800-289-8423)

- Premium-quality lubricant, and lots of it (I recommend Eros®)
- 1 slo-o-ooowww hand

She Brings:
1 pretty nightie, sheer and sexy
1 pretty bottom, squeezed shut
2 pretty eyes, WIDE open!
3 pretty hot spots to tease

*I*n the end, it always pays to be a gentleman.

But there's no denying it – for some reason, every woman finds herself attracted to *bad boys!* There's a dark and deeply **erotic** side to us that occasionally wants a man to dominate us and make us do wicked things. A bad boy can push our sexual buttons in ways no perfectly polite nice guy can.

I learned that lesson again recently when my partner Jeff found a big bag of adult toys I had purchased while doing research for this book. He's a sweetheart, but something about these naughty gadgets brought out the rogue in him, and one night he just... well, he took control. I could hear it in his voice and see it in his eyes. I played along, just like your mate will, and he took me for the ride of my life. You will have to be bold for this **seduction**, perhaps bolder than you've ever been, but your lover will respond to your strength and determination.

"Have I ever told you how much I adore your cute little bum?" After wine and kissing and suitable foreplay, reach up under her nightgown and squeeze her fanny. *"It's true, I love it! In fact, I want to see it right now. Yes, show it to me...."* Put a cushion in front of the sofa, and tell her to kneel and stretch out, bottom in the air. Lift her gown over her hips, and gently massage her bare cheeks. If she tries to move, **spank her**. *"No! I'm not done yet. You stay...."*

Cover your hand with lubricant, and slide your glistening fingers up and down her warm crevasse. Circle the pink rosebud of her anus. Soon, she'll relax enough for your next surprise. It's not a dildo; no, it's much smaller than that. It's called a *butt plug* – soft, gently ribbed, and no wider than your finger. Lubricate it, and tease her tiny sphincter with it. Press it lightly against her anus, then stop. Work the tip in just a fraction of an inch, then pull back. Play with her bottom; watch how it responds. Take your time spreading her tight hole wider, **slipping in and out** and then finally... *push*, until the slightly swollen tip of the plug pops in and stays. Leave it alone for a few minutes while she gets used to this wildly unusual sensation.

In the meantime, bring out another toy. A dildo, yes, but not a big scary one. This one is average in size, and once slicked up will easily slide into her other aroused opening. Gently – *gently!* – move both toys in and out, just an inch at a time. It doesn't take much physical pressure to drive her into a **wild fantasy**. Tell her to turn over on her back. Order her to hold the plug in; command her to spread her legs wide. Now put your mouth between her thighs... and *triple her pleasure*. Move the plug and the dildo, while your tongue flickers across her aching clitoris. Her nerves will be singing, her brain crackling, and in seconds this ultra-bang will launch her into orgasmic overdrive.

Whew! As one who has been taken there by my own very *good* bad boy, I'd like to reemphasize the need to take it easy. With a plug and a **virgin bottom**, a little goes a long way. Like I said at the beginning of this seduction:

In the *end*, it always pays to be a gentle man.

P.S. – About those first five blanks on the invitation –

I suggest you use the following words:	I suggest you do NOT use these:
on	**upside down**
hot	**wash the car**
you Sweetie (use your pet name here)	**"your sister"**
dinner (or lunch, but make sure you do the seduction before you eat. Theres such a thing as feeling too full!)	**"beer"**
meet	**"worship"**

"The only known
aphrodisiac is variety"

-Marc Connolly

I'm going to turn you _____

and then

I'm going to make you _____

and then

I'm going to call _____

and finally

I'm going to fill you up with _____

but first

Get ready to _____ me

Day: _____

Time: _____

Put on
One Extremely Sheer Nightgown
and then meet me in

_____

for a night of passion, lust, and

Erotic Exploration

through Uncharted Sexual Territories

If you are willing to investigate New Pleasures and seek out

Thrills Unknown, then R.S.V.P. one night this week by

approaching me from Behind, pressing your Bare Breasts

against my back, and taking a Bite out of my Neck.

52 Invitations to Grrreat Sex

number 35

Come Out And Play

For Her Eyes Only

"If a man doesn't look at me when I walk into a room, he's gay."

-Kathleen Turner, American Actress

number **35**

Come Out And Play

i n g r e d i e n t s

- 1 large bag
- 2 candles
- Rolling pin
- Self-sealing Baggie
- Roll of plastic food wrap
- Drinking straw

- Massage oil, heated
- 2 spoons, chilled
- Altoids® ("The Curiously Strong Mint")
- Glycerine suppositories (These are *grrreat!* But if ever a product could benefit from a name change and better marketing....)

He Brings
1 flashlight
(Although his grin may be bright enough to read by!)

So many wonderful things happen when you make love. It washes away the tensions of the week and reinforces the bond between partners. It has a way of healing two people, both body and soul.

And it's practically the Fountain of Youth. Let Clinique and Miss Clairol handle the outside; on the inside, there's nothing like an really great **orgasm** to make you feel like a kid again.

But most of all – *sex is fun!* It's a kick to flirt with a man and watch him get interested. It's a big blast to tease him and seduce him and watch him crumble before your irresistible charms. And tumbling around in the buff, touching and rubbing and kissing and licking... well, it's the ultimate party. Elsewhere in this book you'll find **seductions** that emphasize all the other great things sex can do for a relationship – but this one is all about fun.

Do you have a great big purse? How about a large cosmetics bag you don't use any more? Empty it out and fill it with the ingredients on the opposite page. When you lead your lover to the bedroom, he won't be able to miss it; it's prominently displayed on your dresser and flanked by two flickering candles. Give him a sly smile when you explain: *"Oh, every woman has a **bag of tricks** she uses to make sex even better. This is mine."*

Ohhh, yeah; you've got his attention now. *"Would you like to see what I have in store for you tonight? Then give me your flashlight."* Your invitation told him to bring one, and while you have some more interesting plans for it later, right now you're going to use it to illuminate each interesting little object you pull out of your bag.

"Oh, look at this! I'll bet you've never used one in the bedroom before." Show him a zip-lock storage bag. *"Kind of goes with this...."* It's a roll of clear plastic wrap. *"Gosh, maybe we should make love in the kitchen,"* you can **tease** as you pull out a rolling pin. Finally, show him a box of Altoids mints. *"Any guesses? I'll give you a hint. Monica bragged about these to Linda Tripp."* Bingo! One by one, treat him to your special surprises:

The rolling pin makes an extraordinary back massager.

Use a straw to direct a jet of warm air to his nipples, down his belly, and across his **testicles**. Watch his reaction when you blow on his tight little anus!

Hand him his flashlight and invite him to explore your body. He'll be dizzy with excitement while he searches – and memorizes – every erotic inch of you.

Suck on the Altoid, and his penis. (Just as described in the notorious Starr Report. "Presidential knee pads," indeed!)

Fill the Baggie™ with heated massage oil, zip it shut, place it over his penis and stroke.

Pull out two chilled spoons. Tap them against his nipples. Run them between the cheeks of his bottom, followed by **hot kisses**. Use them to cradle his testicles while going down.

"Glad" Wrap takes on a whole new meaning when you coat his erection with lube and then buff his shaft with a slippery sheet of plastic.

Glycerine vaginal suppositories – what a dreadful name for such a fun, sensual product! Pop in one or two and let them melt into a sensational slick lubricant. You might feel a little too wet and goopy... but he'll think he's floating in a big buttery tub of **pure sex**.

So what else can you think of for your bag of tricks? A can of whipped cream? A little Ben-Gay for his buttocks? A Polaroid camera? Oooh, how about a long silk scarf – useful for so many things! A lot of couples run out of fun ideas, but as long as you've got your toys and tricks waiting under the bed, great sex is pretty much guaranteed anytime you want it.

You might say it's *in the bag!*

"*If a man doesn't look at me when I walk into a room, he's gay.*"

-Kathleen Turner, American Actress

You know so much about
Sex!

You know how to turn me on.
You know how to make me hot!
You can make my heart race, and my knees quiver, and my
toes curl, and my thighs tremble.
Your touch makes me wet.

But –

I know some tricks even you don't know!
And I will be happy to demonstrate them all....

Date: _____

Time: _____

Place: _____

For the best possible view, bring one

Flashlight

(and check the batteries! You don't want to be left in the dark.)

R.S.V.P. – check the appropriate answer and return:

_____ *I regret that I am otherwise engaged.*

_____ *I can't wait for you to sit on my face!*

52 Invitations to Grrreat Sex

n u m b e r **36**

The Box $ \$\$ $ 🚗 🍴

For Her Eyes Only

"When I'm good I'm very good,
but when I'm bad I'm better."

-Mae West

n u m b e r 36

The Box

- Dinner
- One box, gift-wrapped
- One fun, fearless female

- One Remote Control Vibrator (If you can't find it at your local adult boutique, check out the Good Vibrations™ catalog. Call 1-800-289-8423 and tell them Laura sent you.)

I guess I'm just an old-fashioned kind of girl.

High-tech wizardry? I'm perfectly happy without it. I don't have a pager, or a cell phone. I view my answering machine with suspicion, and I know just enough about my computer to write these books.

Then I discovered – drum roll, please! – the *Remote Control Vibrator*. Wow! One great big Standing O to the brilliant inventors who came up with this one. This gadget is so much fun, so intriguing, so unbelievably *sexy* that you'll find yourself dreaming up seductions of your own just to have an excuse to use it. But here's how you should introduce it to your lover:

You're in the car – all clean and shiny, per your invitation – and on your way to dinner, when you hand your mate a a tiny, elegantly wrapped package. *"It's for you, honey. You can go ahead and open it, if you want."* At the first red light he pulls the **silk ribbon** and tears the heavy wrapping paper away. Inside the box is a... well, he's not sure what it is. It's a small plastic rectangle with a button on it, something like a garage door opener, but with no signs or instructions. Hmmm....

He pushes the button. And instantly you gasp, back stiffening, eyes closing. He's startled, and turns it off; you relax, sinking into the seat with a little half-smile on your face.

Holy cow! What is this thing?! He's in traffic, and has to pay attention to driving, but his curiosity is burning holes in his psyche. He pushes the button again. And again you gasp, fists clenched, smile broadening, as the delicious tingle of your new toy spreads up through your tummy and out through your thighs. *Ohhhh, yeah* – he's starting to figure it out now. He turns it off, and watches your eyes regain their focus. He turns it on, and this time he notices the gentle hum coming from... why, yes, it really seems to be coming from **under your skirt**! And there's no mistaking the look on your face. He's seen it before. But he's never been able to turn it on by just, literally, turning it on!

By now, his brain is buzzing more than the little radio-controlled gadget strapped under your panties. The whole concept is so wild, so **incredibly erotic**, that he's barely able to grasp the possibilities ahead. One thing is clear already: you love him and trust him enough to give him the power to please you, anytime, anywhere.

But not in the restaurant! Your new friend is perhaps a bit too noisy to use in a crowd, so politely ask for the controller before you go in. Once seated, though, bring it out of your purse and put it right on the table. Tease him with it. Go ahead, punch it up for a couple of seconds when no one's nearby; let him see that glorious expression of **ecstasy** cross your face. He's going to have a very hard time sitting through this meal... with the emphasis on *hard!* Afterward, on the way to the car, let him have his gift again, and this time... well, just enjoy the ride. Let him do whatever he wants. (Of course, what he might want is to break the speed limit on the way home; by now he's had more foreplay than he can stand!)

How about that. Modern science has finally come up with something every woman can use: a remote control for *men*. That's what this really is, you know. Any time you want his attention, just pull out your little box, **squeeze the button**...

...and watch him come running!

"*When I'm good I'm very good,
but when I'm bad I'm better.*"

-Mae West

You are about to explore an

Entirely New Dimension
In Sexuality

which will lead you in directions

unknown in your

Wildest, Wettest Dreams

To prepare for this Erotic Journey, you must:

1) Open Your Mind to a completely new and thrilling Idea

2) Wash and Wax the Car

Your adventure begins this _____ *evening*

at _____ *o'clock*

and includes Dinner, consumed Vertically,

and Dancing, Horizontally

R.S.V.P. with a lick on one hip, a lick on the other, and

then another right in between. No, lower than that. Keep going.

I'll moan when you get there.

52 Invitations to Grrreat Sex

n u m b e r 37

Passion Fuel

FOR HIS EYES ONLY

"Sexuality is not a leisure or part-time activity.
It is a way of being."

-Alexander Lowen

n u m b e r **37**

Passion Fuel

Course 1: Appetizer
Musical Selection:
The Sweetest Taboo –
Sade
• Head To Toe Massage
• Neck & Shoulder Massage
• Foot Massage
• Rolling Pin Massage
• Hot Oil Treatment

Course 4: Chef's Surprise!
Musical Selection:
A 3D Virtual Reality Experience

Course 7: Apéritif
Musical Selection:
You're Making Me High –
Toni Braxton
• Body Spooning
• Slow Dancing
• Candlelight Bubble Bath

Course 2: Specialties Of
The House
Musical Selection:
Time To Say Goodbye –
Andrea Bocelli
• Slow Soft
  Sensuous Kisses
• Hot Talk
• Fingerplay

Course 5: Entreé
Musical Selection:
Principles Of Lust – Enigma
• Rocket Riding
• Tender Thrusting
• Deep "C" Diving

Course 3: Side Dishes
Musical Selection:
Human Beings –
Seal
• Nipple Sucking
• Bottom Tickling
• Neck Nibbling
• Tongue Dueling

Course 6: Dessert
Musical Selection:
Moondance – Van Morrison
• Strawberries & Champagne
• Dark Chocolate
• Cherry Vanilla IceCream

i n g r e d i e n t s

• List of her favorite songs
• 1 special menu (She'll treasure it forever, so make it
  look as nice as you can. Use your computer, or ask
  someone at a print shop to lay it out for you. At the
  very least, type it on elegant paper)
• 1 custom tape or CD (If you can't preprogram the
  songs, then keep the stereo's remote control handy)

• Dessert (You must have everything on the menu
  ready to go)
• Cyborgasm (This extremely erotic CD might be
  found at your favorite adult boutique. If not, call
  Good Vibrations: 1-800-289-8423)

She Brings:
Insatiable appetite
500-star review (that's how many she'll be seeing!)

$\mathcal{E}$very love affair comes with its own soundtrack. Songs we fell in love to, songs we make love to – gosh, Jeff and I even have favorite songs for driving on dates and for cooking in the kitchen. You have special songs, too, don't you? Lyrics you both know by heart... songs that make you melt when you hear the opening notes on the radio... songs that belong to no one else in the world but you.

Songs have **magic** in them. And you're about to use some of that power to treat your lover to a night of passion and pleasure. You're going to *choreograph your lovemaking* to her favorite music.

No, not like a ballet, with every move mapped out. Instead, you're going to match her favorite music to the mood and tempo of the evening. And she's going to help you by telling you what she wants. How? Present her with a menu – **a *sex* menu**!

Your first step is to put together a short list of her favorite songs. You probably know most of them already, but be safe – casually ask her what she likes while you're flipping through the CD collection. Then, sometime when she's not around, make a custom tape for her... or if you've got a multi-disc player, program a set of songs to play in the right order.

Now for the **fun part**! Make a menu that has one song for every course, and under that course, list a few sexual treats for her to choose from. Your menu might look like this: **(see opposite page)**.

On the night of your date, with some sensuous music already filling the air, ask your sweetie to sit down and look over your menu. Tell her to take her time; she'll really enjoy looking over all the options. Hand her a pen and ask her to check off one **erotic treat** under each course. Explain to her that she'll get that special sexual selection for as long as the song lasts. Now pop in your custom mix... and go to work.

Give her that massage, and move with the music while you do it. When the second song starts, begin your next course, kissing and teasing and bopping and grooving and dancing with her horizontally. By the third song, the music should be part of your **lovemaking**; flick your tongue in time with the song, move your cock with the beat. Lick and suck, stroke and squeeze, and play her body like the fine instrument it is, all to the rhythm of her music.

Course four – the **Chef's Surprise** – will blow her away. Play a cut from *Cyborgasm*, an extremely hot CD with sounds of sex, stories of lust, and erotic tales told well. Track 15 is a recording of an orgy, with dozens of people getting aroused and getting off at the same time, and it will absolutely electrify your own lovemaking. Oh, wow, I get **shivers** just writing about it. I think I have to go grab Jeff and the headphones right now.

In the meantime, get to work on your tape. And make some extra copies. It's going to wear out. *And so are you!*

"Sexuality is not a leisure or part-time activity. It is a way of being."

-Alexander Lowen

Indulge your Senses in an Evening of

Gourmet Sex

Your Master Chef has prepared a Menu of Erotic Dishes

from which you may choose anything your heart — and your body — desires.

Would you prefer a 10-minute foot massage to start?

Perhaps a touch of tongue to follow… or something harder?

Whatever you select, you will be served — and serviced — with a smile.

(And even the rare treats will be well-done!)

Date:_____

Location:_____

Your reservations are at _____o'clock

Dress: Casual

Undress: Quickly

No tipping allowed.

(In fact, your waiter has quite a big tip for you!)

R.S.V.P.

If I find a bright red lip print on the windshield of my car…

… I'll take that as a "yes."

52 Invitations to Grrreat Sex

n u m b e r 38

Hard to Resist $

FOR HIS EYES ONLY

"Last time I tried to make love to my wife nothing was happen-
ing, so I said to her, what's the matter,
you can't think of anybody either?"

-Rodney Dangerfield

n u m b e r **38**

Hard to Resist

i n g r e d i e n t s

- A brand new cologne (And, with all due respect to the makers of Old Spice, you do not want a fragrance you can buy in a drug store. Get something more subtle, along with some professional advice: visit a good department store.)

- Spray it on:
  - underwear
  - towel
  - napkins
  - bedding
  - your invitation
  - yourself

She Brings:
1 great smeller
1 great smell
(and 1 great taste!)

"**T**here's something about an Aqua-Velva Man!" *Famous commercial jingle*

When was the last time you went out and bought a new cologne? If you're like most men, the answer is: *practically never*. Right?

The fragrance you wear now was a gift from a woman, wasn't it? Well, there's a lesson in that observation. No, it's not that you stink! (Although, as long as we're on the subject, I can't tell you how many heartbreaking stories I've heard from women who give up on intimacy because of their mate's hygiene problems. Leave it to Corn to step up to the plate and say it out loud! Scrubbed skin, clean hair, fresh breath: it's the uniform you put on *before* the **game of love**.)

The point is this – women smell better. Okay, let me rephrase that! Women smell prettier, sure... but they also *smell* better. Their noses are generally more sensitive than men's. And for reasons scientists are only beginning to understand, scent has a much more powerful effect on women.

You're going to use this fact to knock your mate right off her feet (and right into bed) this week. Your **seduction** begins with a trip to the fragrance bar; you'll find plenty of help in any major department store. You need a really nice, really elegant cologne, which you will use for Phase Two of your seduction – the Big Tease.

Spray a bit of your new fragrance on the invitation before you mail it. Her challenge is to identify it before your big date, and believe me, there's not a woman in America who doesn't think she could do it. Every woman will also recognize this sly twist on an old seduction trick: **spritz a bit** on your boxer shorts, and leave them where she'll find them in her car!

One day when she's stepping out of the shower, greet her with a warm, just-out-of-the-dryer towel lightly scented with... well, you know. Put a dab on the dinner napkins one evening. And when she finally comes to you on the night of your **big date**, make sure there's a hint of your sexy scent on the sheets and pillows.

The object of this game isn't to stump her. No, your plan is to simply sweep her off her feet. You want to put her in a sensual state of mind, to make her extraordinarily *happy* – and that's what a a great fragrance can do for a woman. That's why it's a multi-billion dollar business! Once you're both bare and in bed, and she's been transported by the **heavenly aroma**, ask her if she figured out your challenge.

Chances are she has. Women are really good at this kind of thing. *"Why, congratulations, honey,"* you'll exclaim, as you toss a pillow down on the floor next to the bed. *"You win!"* Kneel on the cushion, grab her ankles and pull her butt to the edge of the bed, right in front of you. *"And your prize"* – lift her legs, push her knees back toward her chest, put her feet on your shoulders – *"is a life-time supply of...mmmph... really enthusiastic ... mm... oral sex...mmm...."*

The scent, and your manly-man way of grabbing her and taking her, and the sudden erotic shock of tongue on clit will have her halfway to orbit. But she may still have the presence of mind to ask the obvious. *"But sweetie... what if I hadn't guessed right?"*

"Mmfl... doesn't matter," you manage between licks. *"I was just... mmmsslurrrp looking for an excuse to get a bit of <u>my</u> favorite fragrance, right here...."*

Now there's a scent any man on the planet would recognize. I've always thought it would make a heck of a weapon, if we could just learn to manufacture it. Spray it over a battlefield and... well, what army can fight with a hundred thousand instant hard-ons?

"Last time I tried to make love to my wife nothing was happening, so I said to her, what's the matter, you can't think of anybody either?"

-Rodney Dangerfield

Do You Know This Fragrance?

Here is your Challenge: You have Five Days in which to
identify this scent. Solve the Mystery and you will be hand-
somely and extravagantly Rewarded

at : _____ o'clock

on the evening of:_____

in your Bedroom

The Prize

will remain a Mystery until then, but you are guaranteed to

like it and derive enormous physical pleasure from it.

The Answer

will remain a Mystery until then, but you are guaranteed to

like it and derive enormous physical pleasure from it.

Your R.S.V.P

must take the form of a gentle Bite on the back of my Neck

within 24 hours of receipt of this Invitation.

52 Invitations to Grrreat Sex

number 39

Worth More Than
A Thousand Words $

For Her Eyes Only

*"Love is not the dying moan of a distant violin -
it's the triumphant twang of a bedspring."*

-S.J. Perelman

n u m b e r **39**

Worth More Than A Thousand Words

i n g r e d i e n t s

- Polaroid™ camera and instant film
- Picture frame with four slots (Make sure it's the right size – bring a test picture when you shop for the frame)
- Quick trip to the cosmetic counter
- Necktie, giftwrapped
- Your nicest suit

He Brings
His Sunday best
His Saturday night wickedest!

Want more sex? Then *think* more sex.

Which simply means that you've got to find ways to make intimacy a priority, along with the other important things in your life. If you're like most couples, your schedule is already jammed. You've got appointments to run, work to attend to, kids to drive here and there, a house to run. And to keep you on track, you might have a calender and a hundred Post-Its™ on your fridge. But what reminds you to have sex?

Well, there's this book, for one thing. Nothing like getting an invitation in the mail! But here's another idea, one I think every loving couple should put into practice:

Pictures. Sensual art on your bedroom walls. Lovely portraits of you and your mate, embracing in soft light. Vacation shots of the two of you, holding hands on a beach. Professional glamour shots, featuring you and a bit of lingerie.

Every time you walk into your bedroom, you should be immediately reminded of the room's central purpose – a place where you two can be your most relaxed and intimate. A place for **sex**. Even if you're only subconsciously aware of them, suggestive pictures will automatically, almost magically, lift sex to its rightful place on your list of priorities.

This week, get your hands on a Polaroid™ camera. Yep, you're going to make some very special pictures to decorate your home. You're also going to need a lovely picture frame, pre-matted to hold a montage of four photos. Oh, and a **necktie**, which – for the very first time in all five of my books – will *actually go around a man's collar!* (You haven't discovered the other wonderful uses of a tie yet? Oh, just keep reading....)

Giftwrap the tie and send it along with your invitation. Get a little makeover at the mall before your big date, and put on your best suit and jewelry. When your slightly bemused but nicely dressed lover arrives, sit him down on the edge of the bed and – *snap!* – take a **pretty picture** of him. Ask him to do the same for you.

Then jump him! This is an afternoon devoted to fun, steamy sex. Let him slip his hands underneath your clothes before you tug them off. **Nibble** every inch of his chest as it's exposed. Turn him onto his tummy and give him a Round-the-World kiss: start at his calves and move up to his bare bottom, concentrating on kissing that erogenous (and so-very-cute!) little crease between his thigh and his butt. Men rarely get special attention to their backs – let's face it, they can be big hairy animals back there – so treat him to a hundred kisses up his spine and around his neck. On the other side, there's so much more to caress and bite and lick and suck, and naturally, the highlight of a Round-the-World tour is a prolonged stop at the North Pole. Or is the South? Well, it's the Pole, and it deserves your finest efforts.

When you're finished, by which I mean when *he's* finished, all flush and sweaty and radiating that unmistakable **post-orgasmic** glow, sit him up again. Throw on his shirt and tie, but leave it all askew, and then snap another photo. You already see where this is going, I'll bet. Uh-huh. It's your turn to enjoy the full erotic attention of the man you love and then – makeup gone, hair a mess, suit jacket barely covering your breasts, and with that wicked just-ravished gleam in your eye – face the camera.

"Before and after," you can tell any of your friends who happen to spot the photos, nestled side by side in the frame. Huh? Before and after... what?

Start silently counting. You can tell a lot about a person by how long it takes for the light bulb to go on over her head. One... two.... *"Oh!"* A smile and a blush spread across her face. *"Before, and after!! Ah-HAH!! Wow. Hmmm. Say, do you still have that Polaroid camera handy?...."*

*"Love is not the dying moan
of a distant violin -
it's the triumphant twang
of a bedspring."*

-S.J. Perelman

I find you
so Attractive
so Strong
so Damn Sexy

And I can't wait to see you wearing this gift...
...with a pressed white shirt...
...your best shoes and slacks...
...and underneath, well...

Surprise Me!

(And oh, by the way, do I have a Surprise waiting for You . . .)

Come Dressed To Kill

Date: _____

Time:_____

Place:_____

R.S.V.P. – with a string of kisses up and down my spine

52 Invitations to Grrreat Sex

n u m b e r 4O

Erector Set $
_____

For Her Eyes Only

"Lovemaking is like the sunset: every day the sun goes down, but every sunset is different."

-Lonnie Barbach, Ph.D.

n u m b e r 40

Erector Set

i n g r e d i e n t s

- 1 long portable mirror
- 1 stepladder (I recommend the traditional kitchen ladder or stool: just three steps and a tall handrail)
- 1 blanket
- 1 pair of sexy shoes

He Brings
1 big white dress shirt
(which you will take and use)
1 big hard erection
(which you will take and use!)

As you go through this book (as well as the three others in my Grrreat Sex series), you're going to accumulate a small collection of basic props that every couple should have in the bedroom. And in terms of sheer bang-for-the-buck, none provide a better value than a *wardrobe mirror*.

You can spend a fortune on an elegant antique in a gilt frame. But the fanciest one in the world is no more fun than a tall, plain, skinny sheet of **mirrored glass** you can get for ten dollars at any Target or Wal-Mart. Don't attach it to your door, though! You want this mirror to go with you, anyplace in the house where you're going to have sex. Put it on its side so you can watch your nude bodies shimmering in front of the fireplace. Lean it against any nearby wall to add a new dimension to lovemaking. For you, it's really hot, and for him it's... oh, absolutely mind-blowing, like watching a fantasy come to life.

Here's another prop you'll need this week: a stepladder. A stool might work, or a small table; what you're looking for is something sturdy you can **climb on**. It should be something that is completely out of place in the bedroom... which is exactly where you're going to put it.

Don't explain what you're up to! You want your lover to be curious – that's the first step towards anticipation, and **anticipation** is the fuel that romance runs on. Two days later, put your big mirror against the wall behind the ladder. By now his curiosity will be at a full simmer.

Thursday, he'll find a soft folded blanket on one of the steps. On Friday, a pair of sexy, strappy shoes appears on another. The sensual mystery finally begins to unfold when he arrives for the big night wearing a big white shirt, which you remove... and then put on yourself, right in front of him. Men just melt at this next move: pull off your **bra and panties** from underneath your clothes. Finally, slip on those slinky shoes, and let the show begin. Climb a few steps up the ladder and pose. Bend forward, grab the rail of the ladder, and thrust your bare bottom straight back. A woman's legs look fabulous in this position, and he won't be able to take his eyes off them. *"Go ahead; kiss them,"* you'll command, and as his lips caress the backs of your thighs, slowly hike the shirttail up over your cheeks. *Mmmm....*

Toss the blanket over one of the steps, then turn around and sit down, with your hips ever-so-conveniently at face level. *"Missed some,"* you tease, while he walks right between your thighs and glides his warm, **wet tongue** over your aching clitoris. This position works just as well in reverse, when *he's* standing on the ladder, watching your pretty mouth bob up and down – and he'll go wild over the view in the mirror.

The ultimate move, the one that really requires a ladder to work well, starts with you back in your first position. Climb back up the ladder, back to your lover, buttocks out. Once his shaft is buried deep inside, you'll have more freedom to move, and more control, than you've ever had before. Twist your hips side to side, or rock up and down, back and forth, **hard and soft**. With the ladder rails to support you, there's nothing you *can't* do to his penis. Go ahead – it can take so much more abuse than you imagine. In fact, the rougher you are, the more explosive his orgasm. And given your position halfway up this miniature Stairway to Heaven, I'd say it's possible that he might blow you, quite literally...

...over the top.

"Lovemaking is like the sunset: every day the sun goes down, but every sunset is different."

-Lonnie Barbach, Ph.D.

A Man Never Looks Better
(and sexier, and yummier!)
than in a
Crisp White Dress Shirt
Starched and freshly pressed.

Too bad you won't be able to keep it on for long.

(I predict you won't keep **anything** *on for long!)*

But wear one anyway. Everytime I see you dressed like that,

I want to _____

And maybe I will...

This _____ *evening at* _____ *o'clock.*

Location: _____

R.S.V.P.

with a long, slow kiss...

...that runs from my left hand to my right...

...and anywhere in between.

52 Invitations to Grrreat Sex

n u m b e r 4I

The Blue Balloon
_____

For His Eyes Only

"To live an erotic life is to follow the bouncing ball, to allow oneself to be distracted and enticed by something playful and childlike. Sex can sometimes be an invitation to the soul to come out and play."

-Thomas Moore, best selling author

number 41

The Blue Balloon

i n g r e d i e n t s

- Six balloons (Bonus points if you get them filled with helium! Otherwise, tape them to the ceiling and let them hang like a piñata.)
- Seven hot sex notes.

- One prick – I mean *pin!* Something to pop the balloons with.
- Champagne (optional)

She Brings:
One blue balloon
One big smile!

"**W**ould you like to fly in my beautiful balloon? Way up in the sky in my beautiful balloon? *"Up, Up, and Away" -The Fifth Dimension*

Who doesn't love a party?

Especially when the dress code is *naked*... and the theme is great sex!

Your lover is to be the guest of honor at just such a party this week. Fortunately, there's not much preparation to go through – the guest list consists of *you*, and the menu is limited to... well, *her*. But you do need to get half a dozen **big red balloons**, some string, and several small sheets of paper.

On the night of the party, she meets you in the kitchen. You hug her, and pop open some champagne or wine. Let the suspense build for a while. She knows you've planned something – she's been thinking about it all week, since she got your invitation – but she hasn't been able to figure out just what it is, and her curiosity is hotter than **her libido**. For the moment, anyway. Finally, you make your announcement. *"I've come up with a great little game to play at our party. Would you like to see it?"* Uh-huh, she would! *"Then come with me...."*

Lead her to the bedroom, where she can't help but notice your balloons. Six of them, blown up and hanging above the bed. *"Inside each balloon,"* you explain, *"is a note. They're all about you... and what I would like to do to you. Go ahead, pop one, and tell me what it says."*

What fun! A little **mystery**, several surprises, a bunch of sex... this is going to be one terrific evening. She takes a pin and – POP! Out floats a note.

*"You have the most beautiful butt in the world. And I am now going to **kiss it**... right after I kiss your neck, your shoulders, and all of your back."*

Yep, this party is definitely showing signs of life. Next balloon – POP! *"Poor baby; you've been on your feet all day. I am going to give them the best massage they have ever had, starting with your toes and moving up until you say stop."*

Oh, yeah. This is the kind of party a girl can get used to. And there are still so many balloons left! POP – *"Show me those **magnificent breasts**... and I will show you how I can worship them."* POP! – *"I have massage oil, and ten strong fingers. Got any place that needs some serious rubbing?"*

POP! – *"You are the sexiest woman alive, and I am now going to place my mouth between your thighs and suck you until you come."* Ohhhh, wow. This party was worth the wait. This might have to become a monthly affair.

Later, as you're both catching your breath and basking in that toasty post-orgasmic glow, a question will float to the surface of her thoughts. *"Hey, your invitation asked me to bring this blue balloon. I thought you were maybe going to put it on **Mr. Happy** here, or something! What's it for?"*

At that moment, you reach for one last note, hidden in your night stand. Insert it into her balloon, blow it, tie it off with string, and hang it from the ceiling. *"That,"* you'll say with a sly smile, *"is for me to know, and for you to find out."* Huh?!

*"It's something I've been **dying for** you to do for me. Just thinking about it gets me hot! But you can't pop the balloon until I say so."*

So what is it? That's up to you, of course. A slinky striptease? A slow scrub in the shower? An evening drive with her skirt hiked high and her fingers busy? Whatever it is, one thing is certain. After three or four days of staring at that balloon, knowing that it contains the secret of your erotic fantasy – she's going to be ready to POP!

"To live an erotic life is to follow the bouncing ball, to allow oneself to be distracted and enticed by something playful and childlike. Sex can sometimes be an invitation to the soul to come out and play."

-Thomas Moore, best selling author

It's a Party!

And since You are the

Guest of Honor

you are expected to come

and come and come and come and come

and come and come and come and come

Date: _____

Time: _____

Place: _____

Dress: practically naked

Orgasms and drinks are on the house.

You are, however, requested to bring

One Blue Balloon, not inflated,

and never previously used

R.S.V.P.

If, one evening after work, I see you on the sofa with your

knees slightly parted, your skirt slightly raised, and your fin-

gers gently stroking the sheer fabric of your panties…

I'll take that as a yes.

52 Invitations to Grrreat Sex

n u m b e r **42**

Sex In A Secret Place

For Her Eyes Only

"People who are sensible about love are incapable of it."

-Douglas Yates

n u m b e r **42**

Sex In A Secret Place

i n g r e d i e n t s

- 1 public place that can be locked
- 1 note

- 1 gym bag (with blanket and hygiene supplies)

He Brings
1 candle
1 lighter
1 very big bang
1 very short fuse!

So how many places have you done it outside your home?

I hear it time and time again, on my radio shows and in my surveys: men and women get a huge erotic rush out of sneaking a quickie in a semi-public place. One of the most popular seductions in my *101 Nights of Grrreat Sex* is called "**The Secret Dessert.**" In it, our lucky couple goes to an elegant restaurant... and then sneaks off to the restroom between courses! Oh, if I just had the tip from every nice meal that seduction has sold....

Of course, no one really wants to get caught – literally! – with their pants down in public. But it is possible to capture the thrill of spontaneous, do-me-now, **on-the-spot sex** without a lot of real risk. All it takes is a bit of forethought. So let me rephrase my opening question: how many places *could* you do it outside your home?

Keep your eyes open this week. Start making a special list of all the public rooms you come across that can be locked without raising suspicion. Offices... closets... dressing rooms. Check out "Beat Around The Bush" in my *Grrreat Sex* book for a steamy seduction in the great outdoors! But it's the **public restroom** that gets the highest marks from my readers. They have two big advantages – they're everywhere, and they're usually hidden just enough so that you can both pop in without drawing attention. How about the one at the gym? Your favorite nightclub? Ooh, here's an idea that's a little safer yet still really hot: *your best friend's house.* I'd love to show you *my* very favorite spot – it's about a mile from my house – but the manager might be reading this book! (Could be trouble, but... hmm... maybe I'd get better service if he knew.) Your own special surprise will go something like this:

Your lover is already excited as you climb into the car. Your invitation made it clear that he's going to get some today, but he has no idea when or where. Nothing seems out of the ordinary when you stop at a **gas station** along the way. But imagine the stunned look on his face when he reads the note you hand him: *"Ladies Room. Exactly two minutes. Bring the scented candle and my very favorite penis. I'm going to ignite them both."*

Grab your gym bag out of the trunk and get the key from the attendant. Once inside, pull a blanket from the bag and drape it over the sink. Panties in the bag, bottom against the sink, legs slightly apart, skirt up. When your mate walks through the door, make **your demands** short and to the point. *"Lock the door. Light the candle. Come here and do me."* The scent of vanilla fills the room, not quite masking the aroma of arousal. Lock lips while you tug at his zipper; reach into his pants and grab his rapidly swelling penis. Stroke it hard and fast, and as soon as it reaches its full size, rub the head against your moist lips. Let your juices flow onto the tip of his proud manhood and then, as quickly as you can, slip it inside. Wrap one leg around his hip and pull him deeper.

Outside your **private heaven**, people are going about their business, with no idea that something so hot, so nasty, is happening just a few feet away. And they'd be so shocked – no, so *jealous* – if they only knew. For a few moments you're going at it with all the energy and electricity of a couple of adolescents, and your body is responding with the kind of energy you had in your first few months together. The sheer animal power of a **public quickie** is... overwhelming. Addictive, even.

You *did* keep that list, didn't you?

"People who are sensible about love are incapable of it."

-Douglas Yates

You Will Not Know When . . .
You Will Not Know Where . . .
But sometime soon you are going to
Get Lucky and
Get Off

Yes, there is Sex in your immediate future, and so,

like a good Boy Scout, you must

Be Prepared —

Which means you should be Clean in Mind, Body, and BVD's.

And for this particular adventure you will need

One Vanilla-Scented Candle *(with lighter)*

which you must keep with you at all times *in preparation for*

Immediate and On-The-Spot Sex.

*The day is*_____

Don't even try to guess the time and place.

R.S.V.P. To accept, simply bend over...

... and moon me!

52 Invitations to Grrreat Sex

n u m b e r 43

Extreme Foreplay

For His Eyes Only

"Passive people never live passionate lives."
-Anonymous

n u m b e r 43

Extreme Foreplay

i n g r e d i e n t s

• Big, comfortable chair
• Smooth, soft nylon rope (I got mine at Target)

• Lots of candles

She Brings:
Short skirt
Short struggle
Long surrender

Okay, I admit it. We don't know what we want.

Women, I mean. We're walking contradictions. Torn between duty and desire. We're raised to be responsible, to care for kids, to turn boys into men, to be *good girls*. We have to be in control. And yet....

The number three fantasy for women is being **sexually dominated**. Those romance stories we buy by the millions are called "bodice-rippers" in the book business, because almost all of them end with a strong man tearing the heroine's clothes off and having his way with her. We can totally indulge in sensual pleasure and still be "good girls" only if our lovers *take control away from us* and make us do all the carnal, nasty things we secretly crave. Your sweetie may have been afraid to talk about domination, but trust me – she dreams about it.

This week, her dreams come true. As instructed, she meets you in the bedroom wearing a black lace bra, black skirt, and **black panties**. In the center of the room is a large, comfy chair, with a big pillow leaning against the back. Invite her to sit. Talk with her as you walk around the room, lighting one candle, then another, and then turning off the lamps. *"Step one, my love. Pull off those panties...."*

Hidden somewhere out of view is a *lasso* – a slick, soft nylon rope, like rock climbers use, with a big loop tied at one end. Stand behind her so she can't see it. Toss the loop over her, then quickly wrap the rope several times around her torso, gently **binding her** to the chair. Another length of rope ties her ankles to the legs of the chair, pulling her thighs apart. She may squeal and giggle and object at first, but the noise will stop when she sees you begin to undress. She'll be quite attentive when you free your penis from your boxers. She'll be hypnotized when you start to stroke it.

Play with her, too. Roll her nipples between your fingers. They're hard, aren't they? Uncover her **breasts** and kiss them. Slide the smooth, silky cord over them, back and forth, as a reminder of her helpless position.

Kneel between her open legs. The pillow behind her back pushes her butt to the edge of the seat. Lick her. Flick your tongue across her **swollen clit** until she she's just about ready to pop and then – *stop*.

Stand up and kiss her while tweaking one nipple. Give her a little taste of your erection. Just a minute or two and then – *stop*. Kneel again. Touch her, stroke her, jerk her off with your fingers. Bring her to the edge of orgasm, and then – *stop*. Make love to her mouth again, but only for a minute or two, and then – drop to your knees and circle her **aching clitoris** with your tongue. Slip one wet finger in, just a couple of inches. Curve it up in a little "come-hither" move and rub it against her G-spot; tap-tap-tapping inside while you suck her clit outside. Start the cycle again. Eat her until she's ready to explode; ride her mouth until *you're* ready to explode. Finally, give her permission to come. *Order* her to come, and don't stop until she does.

She's exhausted; limp as a rag doll. Completely unable to resist as you untie her and turn her over, face down on the chair, **bare bottom** open to your pounding shaft. She's helpless... pinned... totally dominated. Totally willing to be your toy, happy to receive a sex-slave's thrashing as your hips slap against her cheeks, completely ready for you to fill her and fulfill her.

I mentioned that this is the third most popular woman's fantasy. Number one? Sorry, can't help you. You don't need a book, you need another *person*. As for number two, well, it's on the way. And here's a hint:

Hang on to that rope.

"Passive people never live passionate lives."

-Anonymous

Black

Black skirt. Black panties. Black bra.
That is the uniform you must wear when you
enter my new contest.

Players

You and Me.

Prize

Two breathtaking, toe-curling, back-arching orgasms.
One is mine. Play by the rules, and you can win the other.

Rules

There are no rules. There is only my whim.
Are you woman enough to handle it?

Date: _____

Time: _____

Place: _____

R.S.V.P.

To signal your acceptance of this challenge,
leave the envelope in which this invitation arrived
on my dresser. In it, place a small locket of hair.

Not, however, from your head.

52 Invitations to Grrreat Sex

n u m b e r 44

Sugar Buzz

For Her Eyes Only

"The right diet directs sexual energy into the parts that matter."

-Barbara Cartland

n u m b e r **44**

Sugar Buzz

i n g r e d i e n t s

- Grapes
- Strawberries
- Any other small fruit you like, strung together into belts and necklaces
- Banana

- Whipped cream
- Bowl
- Robe
- Candles
- Dinner

He Brings:
Music, for dancing
Mouth, for nibbling
Other parts, also for nibbling

Sex does a lot of good things in a relationship. It binds two people on a spiritual level, it lowers the barriers to communication, it frees the mind and banishes stress. This particular seduction does all that, of course, and it offers one rather unusual extra feature:

It's part of a well-balanced diet! Yep, you're going to get your Minimum Recommended Daily Allowance of sensual pleasure *and* Vitamin C this week.

When I was doing research for this book, I came across a beautifully illustrated cookbook called Intercourses, which is all about – you guessed it – **food and sex**. One of the pictures was startling; funny and so-o-o-ooo sexy at the same time. A nude woman was dancing a hula... but her "grass" skirt was made of asparagus! (Yes, it was a very short skirt.) Well, my favorite seductions are the ones that can make Jeff laugh while turning him on, so I came up with this yummy plan. (And I hope you have as much fun with it as I did!)

Start with a cozy dinner for two. Your sweetie will be bringing a new CD to the party, but don't put it on just yet. Keep him in suspense through the salad and main course. Finally, when dinner's over – but before dessert – give him his **instructions**. He is to stay in the kitchen exactly five minutes, then go to the bedroom and start the music. He must sit on the edge of the bed... and wait.

In the meantime, you light the candles in the bedroom, then disappear into the bath where you prepare your surprise. After the music starts, you come out, dressed only in a bathrobe... well, not *only* in a robe, but your **special accessories** are hidden at first. Smile at him, and begin to dance. Trust, he won't care how well you dance! Just smile and move to the music. Whirl, and shake, and then lean in and let him see what's dangling around your neck. Why, they're grapes, strung together on a thread like pearls. Once he's picked his jaw up off the floor, encourage him to take a bite.

Let your robe fall open, revealing the three ripe strawberries, pierced through with needle and thread and dangling low on your hips. There's a bowl on your nightstand, and in it, a can of whipped cream. Grab it and squirt a tiny daub onto each berry. And then another one below that... and another one below *that*, right on your favorite spot, letting him **nibble and lick** and follow your trail with his tongue.

Don't worry; you get some dessert, too. Playfully undress him, then whirl and grab another item from your bowl. Slide down between his thighs and then slowly, seductively raise a banana, right next to his own, uh, banana, and pull back the peel. I don't have to tell you what to do with it, do I? Put on a real show for him, **devouring** this phallic symbol as seductively as possible, and then shift your attention to the real thing right in front of you. When you start to feel the distant rumblings of his erotic explosion, climb up in his lap, slide him inside and hold on.

And congratulations! You are now one of the rare and lucky women who will never have any trouble getting her man to do some grocery shopping. *"Honey, would you mind stopping at the store for a few things?"* Give him a wink and a smile. *"I feel like making a little fruit salad for dinner tonight!"*

*"The right diet directs
sexual energy into
the parts that matter."*

-Barbara Cartland

An Evening Of Sensual Pleasure Awaits

You will find yourself consumed by love

(and consumed by your lover)

if you can attend an evening of

Dinner

Dancing

and extremely sensual Romancing

this _____ evening at _____ o'clock.

To make the evening complete, you are asked to bring the Music,

in the form of a new recording of your choice.

Come hungry. Come on time. Come.

(In that order!)

52 Invitations to Grrreat Sex

n u m b e r 4 5

The Trickster

FOR HIS EYES ONLY

"French kissing is not a tongue-to-tonsils regatta.
Try swallowing first and don't go shoving your tongue down your partner's throat.
Pretend your tongue is Barishnakov instead of Rambo and you will do just fine. Keep
in mind that mouths, like numerous other body parts, enjoy variety!"

-Paul Joannides, author of the very cool,
The Guide To Getting It On!

n u m b e r 45

The Trickster

i n g r e d i e n t s

- 1 pillowcase
- 1 ribbon
- Surgical gloves (available at any drug store)
- String
- 1 new toothbrush
- 1 strong bathrobe sash (or a large towel)

- Menthol cough drops
- Small hand mirror
- Dice
- Body paint (optional)
- Vibrator (mandatory)
- Showmanship (essential!)

She Brings:
Scissors
The audience, and the stage, for the Mr. Trickster Show

Yeah, yeah, I know. Sex is a deeply spiritual experience. Bonding, intimacy, healing, self-esteem, etcetera. Hey, you don't have to tell me; I wrote the book!

All those things are true, of course, but more important than any of them: *sex is fun!* Great big jiggling Jell-O tubs of fun! So much fun that we keep getting drawn back to it, and are thereby exposed to the healing and connection and all those other good things. Those are **explored** elsewhere in the book, but this week... the agenda is pure entertainment.

Your lover will laugh when she walks into your living room and sees a large pillowcase sitting on the coffee table, with the open end tied up with **ribbon**. *"What's that? Why, it's my <u>bag of tricks</u>! It's just full of little surprises, and they all have to do with – you guessed it – SEX. Would you like to see what's inside?"*

You bet she would! Use her scissors to cut the ribbon, and make a big production of opening the pillowcase. *"Oooh, what do you suppose this might be for?"* you'll ask, as you pull out a toothbrush, still in it's factory-sealed package. *"Hmmm... how about this? Any idea what I'm going to do with this?"* Pull out a length of string... and whatever she guesses, tell her <u>no</u> before putting it in the bag. *"Ahh, here's something you'll recognize...."* It's a pair of dice. Bounce them in your hand. *"Interested in a little game of chance? Yes? Then come with me...."*

Throw the bag over your shoulder like Santa on Viagra, and lead her to the **bedroom**. One by one, pull out your tricks and have some fun, starting with the dice. They're *strip dice,* and each number you roll means you have to take off one item of clothing. Here's a suggestion:

2. Shirt	6. Panties or briefs	10. Skirt or dress
3. Belt	7. Pants	11. Shoes
4. Socks or stockings	8. Jewelry	12. **Wild card!** Anything your
5. Bra	9. Watch	opponent wants

First one naked loses. Or wins! Doesn't matter. Move on to your other tricks:

String... which you loop around one raised nipple. *Gently* tug on her tender aureole. Lasso her other nipple as well, then – easy now! – make her breasts dance like happy little sex puppets.

Menthol cough drops – for an extra zing when you "eat at the Y."

Put a vibrator directly against your chin (or the underside of your tongue) while going down. Turn your entire mouth into a **3-volt sex toy**!

Latex surgical gloves... which make a delightfully wicked *snap* when you pull them on. *"Ready to play 'Doctor,' my dear?"* Coat them liberally with a water-based lubricant and give her the genital massage of her life. Flutter over her clit, massage her G-Spot. Send the slippery smooth tip of one wet little pinkie dancing through that tiny, tight back door....

A toothbrush, which may make her giggle at first... but just wait until she feels what it does! Rub the bristles along the crease between thigh and butt; use the handle to massage her labia and spank her vulva. If she's up to it, lightly scratch the skin to either side of her clitoral hood.

A thick bathrobe sash (or a heavy towel, rolled up): Approach her from behind as she bends over – *woof woof!* – and pass it under her hips. The ends of the sash are her "**reins**;" grab 'em, pull her close, and hang on for a wild ride! She'll love the totally helpless, totally penetrated feeling of being trapped against your penis, unable to escape. (Especially if you can lift her off her knees!)

What else can you think of to put in your Bag O' Tricks? A mirror, so she can get your view of penetration? Glow-in-the-dark body paint? How about and actual *pillow?* Not for her head – for her hips. You certainly wouldn't want to sleep on this pillowcase.

But you'll both sleep better *because* of it!

"French kissing is not a tongue-to-tonsils regatta. Try swallowing first and don't go shoving your tongue down your partner's throat. Pretend your tongue is Barishnakov instead of Rambo and you will do just fine. Keep in mind that mouths, like numerous other body parts, enjoy variety!"

-Paul Joannides, author of the very cool, *The Guide To Getting It On!*

It's like getting an extra

Birthday Party!

But instead of marking a passing year

We're going to celebrate

Your Body —

All its glorious, beautiful parts

All its wonderful, sexy pieces

And the way they all work together to create

Joy, Arousal, Lust, Heat, Tingles, Sensual Pleasure

and those incredible window-rattling Orgasms.

And that's just in Me! So try to imagine the treats

I have in store for You…

To find out, please bring

A Pair Of Scissors

This _____ evening

Location:_____

Time:_____

R.S.V.P. — Will you be able to attend?

If, one evening at dinner, I feel a bare foot creeping under the

table, into my lap and then snuggling against my cojones…

… I'll take that as a "yes.…"

52 Invitations to Grrreat Sex

n u m b e r 46

Love Juices And Other Squeezables

For Her Eyes Only

*"Love and intimacy can grow stale when taken for granted.
Innovation is its own reward. Even the best gourmet dinner
can get boring if it's served night after night."*

-Lonnie Barbach, Ph.D.

n u m b e r **46**

Love Juices And Other Squeezables

i n g r e d i e n t s

- 1 serving bowl
- 1 small knife

- 3 large oranges (or, if your lover is especially endowed, 3 grapefruits)

He Brings:
Four towels
Daily dose of Vitamin P (So good for you – and goes down easy!)

Sex can be just so... *messy.*

(If you're doing it right, that is!)

And I don't think I've ever found a messier way to have really fun, really *grrreat* sex than this seduction, which is why I suggest you plan it for a Saturday morning when you have some time to play, and time to jump in the shower. Your lover will be providing the towels – four great big fluffy ones, according to your invitation – so he'll suspect you've planned something **a little wet**. But this treat goes way beyond wet. This one is positively *juicy.*

Do you like to tease your mate? Then, by all means, go ahead and greet him at the bedroom door while **smiling**... *and waving a knife.* Watch the color drain from his face! *"Oh, don't be nervous; this isn't for you! Unless you've done something bad lately. Have you? Is there something I should know about? Hmm?"*

I know some women who would think this is the greatest joke in the world! (And, uh, well, maybe I'm one of them. I've been told I have a pretty wicked sense of humor!) For most of us, though, it's a better idea to wait until your lover is **bare** and comfortable on the bed before bringing out the knife. And don't make any Lorena Bobbitt jokes; you don't want to scare him off before the fun starts.

After some kissing and rubbing and rolling around, go to your nightstand, where you've left a serving bowl with three large oranges. Slip the knife into one and slowly carve a hole in the end, stopping occasionally to lap up the running juice as **seductively** as you can. Make sure your man is sitting on one of the towels, then move between his legs and start to squeeze the nectar out onto his swelling erection.

Did I mention that these have to *room-temperature* oranges?

Don't be shy about **licking** the juice. Make noise; *slurp* it up. Grab another orange and quarter it; squeeze each wedge over his scrotum and his stiff and throbbing manhood. Suck every drop. Follow every sweet rivulet with your tongue. And then, when he's hot, and hard, and close to popping...

... grab the first orange again, place the hole right over the tip of his engorged shaft, and *push.* (Did I mention that it had to be a *large* hole?) Thrust his erection deep into the soft, squishy fruit, and squeeze the orange some more. Slowly twist it and turn it, mashing it into him; bounce it up and down. Use it as if it were another mouth, while your tongue **chases** the pulp and juice running down toward your thighs. Let him see the nectar spilling over your lips and down your chin; it's an erotic image that will stay with him forever. (And one that will certainly pop back into his head next time you're walking through the produce section of the grocery store! Which might make for an awfully interesting shopping trip....)

You haven't forgotten about that third orange, have you? This one gets sliced in half, and once you start to squirt the juice onto **your breasts** and between your thighs (while laying on another towel, of course), he'll get the idea. And there are still two more clean towels waiting for you, which leads me to Laura Corn's *Rule Of Extremely Messy Sex:*

Cleaning up is half the fun!

"Love and intimacy can grow stale when taken for granted. Innovation is its own reward. Even the best gourmet dinner can get boring if it's served night after night."

-Lonnie Barbach, Ph.D.

Good, Clean Fun

is definitely Not on the agenda for this weekend.

You are hereby invited to join your sweetheart for a morning of

Carnal Pleasure – which will be Good, and

Orgasms Galore – which will be Fun

But there will be nothing particularly Clean about this round of

heart-pounding, head-spinning, buttocks-clenching Sex,

which is why you are required to bring the following:

Four (4) Great Big Fluffy Towels

Day: _____

Time: _____

Location: _____

R.S.V.P.

If you will be able to come -

and you will; oh yes, you will - please leave

one bar of scented French-milled Soap

on the kitchen table.

52 Invitations to Grrreat Sex

number 47

Hidden Talent

For Her Eyes Only

"Having frequent sex does very much more than release tensions. It raises your self-esteem; it re-establishes your closeness with your partner; it defines your status as a woman; it demonstrates that somebody needs you and desires you...not just every now and then...but all the time."

-Graham Masterton

number 47

Hidden Talent

Course 1: Appetizer
Musical Selection:
Con Te Partiro –
Andrea Bocelli
- Shoulder, Neck &
  Back Massage
- Rolling Pin Massage
- Head-to-Toe Breast
  Massage

Course 2: Specialties Of
The House
Musical Selection:
Counting Crows
- Slow Sensuous Striptease (Note:
  in mine, I left on panties, high
  heels... and lots of jewelry!)
- Lap Dance
- Football. My feet, your balls!

Course 3: Side Dishes
Musical Selection:
Midnight Tango – Al DiMeola
(7-minute version)
- Honey Dripping (followed by
  Honey Licking)
- Nipple Nibbles
- Monkey Spanking
- Pick any number between 68
  and 70

Course 4: Entrée
Musical Selection:
Principles Of Lust – Enigma
- The Screaming Missionary
- La-Z-Boy Recliner
- Knob Bobbing
- Pin The Tail
(And remember to squeeze squeeze
SQUEEZE to the beat of the
music!)

Course 5: Dessert
Musical Selection:
A Tribute To A Rose – Jimmy
Ponder
- Cognac & Coffee
- Strawberries & Whipped Cream
- Hot Tea & Honey

Course 6: Apéritif
Musical Selection:
Time To Say Goodbye – Sarah
Brightman
- Rubdown with Steamed
  Washcloth
- Candlelight Shower For Two
- Spooning to Dreamland

i n g r e d i e n t s

- List of his favorite songs
- 1 special menu (This will be a keepsake, so make it
  look nice. Use your computer and some elegant paper,
  or write it out as neatly as you can.)
- 1 custom tape or CD (If you can't preprogram
  the songs, keep the stereo's remote control handy)

- Dessert (You don't know what he'll pick, so be prepared to serve everything on your menu)
- 1 strong *squeeze* (To practice, take a tinkle and
  squeeze until you cut off the flow; repeat several
  times. That same motion clamps your vagina around
  his penis, which also causes his eyeballs to roll – and
  his wallet to relax!)

He Brings
Your favorite dance partner

*T*here's magic in music.

You know that already, of course; I'll bet you and your sweetheart had an entire soundtrack of your own when you first fell in love – songs you danced to, songs you played in bed. Even now your heart races when you hear them, I'm sure.

I hope you still surround your relationship with music. And I hope you still make time to dance, even if it's just a whirl around the kitchen. A lot of couples don't, sadly; music seems to be one of the things that falls by the wayside after a while. But as you're about to prove, favorite songs never lose their power to generate **passion**. And when it comes to dancing, well... your mate will be blown away when you show him how to boogie to The Squeeze!

The Squeeze is the technique in which you contract your PC muscles during intercourse, creating a fabulous tight gripping sensation around your man's penis. But this week it's the world's most sensual dance step; you're going to *squeeze your lover to the rhythm of the music.*

His music, to be precise. Your whole **erotic evening** will be choreographed to your sweetie's favorite songs. First, you have to find out what they are, but try not to tip your hand when you ask. Next, make a custom tape of his tunes. And finally, create a *menu* for your seduction.

This will be fun! Your menu will list several courses, and each course will have one special song that goes with it. Under each course will be a multiple-choice selection of sexual treats, customized to his taste. As an example, here's what mine looked like when I did this for Jeff: **(see opposite page)**.

When your lover arrives, ask him to look over the menu for the evening – and watch his smile when he sees what you've been planning! Explain that he can choose one special **sexual treat** for each course, which will last as long as the song plays. Once he's finished, pop in your custom mix, turn the music up... and turn your lover on.

Dance while you stroke him; let him admire your body as you bounce to the beat. Turn every song into a show. Kiss and **fondle** and suck and lick and do it to the rhythm of the music. Merengue on his mouth, Two-Step on his tongue. Turn sex into a swing dance, jumping and jiving while you give him everything he asked for.

And when he's inside you, do the *Squeeze*. Clamp those muscles tight, as if you could snap his shaft off at the base. Squeeze two three four, squeeze two three four; rock your hips, rock your hips, lift and squeeze. Make him feel the music's **pulse** in his cock and in his soul.

When it's all over, and you've both caught your breath, hand your sweetie the cassette with your hot soundtrack. But keep an extra copy hidden; this one will wear out pretty fast.

And if you've done your job right... *so will he!*

"Having frequent sex does very much more than release tensions. It raises your self-esteem; it re-establishes your closeness with your partner; it defines your status as a woman; it demonstrates that somebody needs you and desires you...not just every now and then...but all the time."

-Graham Masterton

May I Have This Dance?

I've got a sexy new step to show you

You'll find it easy to learn: I'll take the lead.

You'll find it easy to do: the moves are all mine.

You'll find it easy to dress for: the costume is skin.

But mostly you'll find: I'm easy!

Come work up a sweat with me...

...horizontally...

Date: _____

Time: _____

Place: _____

I'm going to teach you a whole new meaning to the word "ballroom...."

R.S.V.P.

Shower my tummy with kisses,

then put your mouth on my bellybutton...

...and pbpbpbzlzlzlbrrraatttt BLOW

until I can't giggle any more!

52 Invitations to Grrreat Sex

n u m b e r 48

Head Games

For His Eyes Only

*"If you can express what you really need
and want without fear and shame, your desires are
often met with surprising quickness."*

-Alexander Penny

n u m b e r 48

_____

Head Games

i n g r e d i e n t s

• Game stores or your favorite adult boutique
should be able to get these for you:
• Dirty Minds™ (TDC Games, Inc. Item #1040
www.TDCGames.com)
• Sexual Trivia®
(Matscot International Item #77333)

• Romantic Rendezvous™
(Relationship Enrichment Systems Item # 2222)
• And the rest...Candles Wine or other beverage
• Blanket

_____

She Brings:
Your prize!

I'll bet you saw that title and thought you were going to get a blow job!

Well... *maybe*. Hang on, we'll get to that.

No, this seduction is about other games – the kind you need a ***good head*** to win! I mean word games, specifically, and I include them here in order to make two points. One: for women, words are powerful. Sexual. We can be turned on with the right words. In fact, there are five or six adventures in this book that focus on the seductive power of language. And two: presentation is everything. At least half the success of any seduction is in the setup.

Who knows why? It's just one of those fundamental differences between the sexes, I guess. It's a bit of a generalization, I know, but woman come to bed for the foreplay, and men for... well, for the blowjobs. (Hang *on*, I said! It's on the way.) To put it a little more accurately, everybody loves an orgasm, but everybody gets to it in their own way – and with women, you can't go wrong by starting with *candles and a **picnic in bed***.

Make your bedroom look really nice and she'll be knocked out, as much by the effort as by the beauty of the scene. Light four or five scented candles before she arrives for your date. Throw an extra blanket on top of the bed, and set up a tray with a few snacks and a couple of drinks. In the center of it all, place one of my favorite word games. It's called Dirty Minds™... and believe it or not, it's not about sex! Not exactly, anyway. The object of the game is to come up with *clean* answers using some very suggestive clues. Here's an example:

You read the following to your lover: *"My balls get shot off."* Huh?!! There's a clean answer to that? She gives up, so you read the next clue. *"A **stiff rod** gets me ready."* Oh, come on! That's gotta be dirty! Final clue: *"I sometimes have a man inside me."* If she's clever, she may figure it out – it's a cannon! And so she gets to draw a card and take a turn.

Now she hits you with a clue: *"All day long, it's in and out."* Hmmm... tough one. The more clues you need, the fewer points you get. *"I discharge loads from my shaft."* Eee-yeww! Gross! And also no help. *"Both men and women go down on me."* Get it yet?

It's an elevator! And so it goes.

The game is a blast; I giggle myself silly every time I play it. Your sweetie will, too, but at the same time, something else will be happening, something very special. *She'll be **thinking about sex***. The words work their magic, setting up a little telegraph between her brain and her clit. One tickles the other, back and forth, slowly raising her temperature... and her nipples!

Here's another game that will do the same – it's called Sexual Trivia® and you advance around the board by answering some **pretty wild** questions. It covers everything from the obscure (how many calories in a normal ejaculate?) to the surprising (which New York Yankee was charged with bigamy?) to the bizarre (how much does an elephant penis weigh?).

Of course, wordplay is only a part of foreplay. So kiss while you're playing. Touch while you're laughing: *"Buzz! Wrong answer – time to tweak your nipple!"* After a glass or two of wine and a couple of warmup rounds, offer to make it a little more interesting. Place a bet. Not for money – for *time*. Say, twenty minutes of whatever the winner wants in bed. Hey, I told you we'd eventually get to the blow jobs! But even if she beats you, you're going to love losing this game, or my name isn't...

... well, you figure it out: *it's hard to eat me without teeth. A little oil gets me heated up. Pulling my ears gets me off!!*

"If you can express what you really need and want without fear and shame, your desires are often met with surprising quickness."

-Alexander Penny

I have a few
Questions for you —

You may have seen Jeopardy.

You have played Trivial Pursuit.

Well, turn up the heat, throw in some body contact,

set the controls to "wicked," and

you'll have an inkling of what's in store when we play:

E. 2.

The Erotica Quiz!

Test your Bedroom Knowledge...

Challenge your Opponent's Skills...

Gamble with Sensual Pleasures...

This is the Quiz Show that you'll _Want_ to go into Overtime,

and it starts at _____ o'clock this _____ night.

Location: _____

Your buzzer awaits (batteries charged!)

R.S.V.P.

Simply fill out the following, and return:

_____ Regrettably, I must decline

_____ Just thinking about it makes me wet. I'll be there.

(And I'm going to kick your butt!)

52 Invitations to Grrreat Sex

n u m b e r 49

Deep C Diver $

For Her Eyes Only

"Soon I felt her mouth. I had still a sort of semi hard on. She got it into her mouth and she began to caress it with her tongue. I saw stars."

-Henry Miller, Tropic of Capricorn

number **49**

Deep C Diver

ingredients

• 1 Thera-Band Ball™ (They look like heavy-duty beach balls and can support 1000 pounds. Buy it at an exercise equipment store, or call Fitness Wholesale: 1-800-537-5512. Match it to your body size: mine is 26 inches and cost $18.50; the biggest ones are only $39.95. *You are going to love it!* Sex positions galore – I still haven't discovered all the wonderful uses for this toy. I keep it in the corner of my bedroom, always reminding us to come back and try some more.)

Deep oral action (Try a Creme de Menthe blow job! Use a small mouthful of the green liquor to coat his erection. Exhale over his penis for an exquisite blast of warmth. Inhale for a thrilling chill. Suck hard for a happy lover!)

He Brings

1 sexy movie (I suggest the classic Deep Throat) or another treat of your choosing

2 balls (These won't support any weight. But they can lift him clear off the ground!)

You are about to learn my favorite new trick for performing oral sex.

This is a topic to which I have devoted myself for years, and not because I write these books, or give advice to women on the radio, or even because Jeff likes it so much. No, the simple truth is that I adore it. I love it! I love everything about **fellatio** – the feel of it, the look of it, the reaction to it (!!), and especially the incredible, intense intimacy of it. Oh, and the power: do it right and you *own* your lover.

Out of all the ways to do it, the best is the technique commonly known as Deep Throat. Did you ever see the movie of the same name? I'll never forget it. *Wow.* I was completely blown away by Linda Lovelace's oral skills in that film, and so I'm going to encourage you and your mate to watch it. BUT... I know that many people are uncomfortable with **adult videos**, and that's why I left a blank line at the bottom of this week's invitation. If you're up to it, ask your lover to rent a copy and bring it home as a sort of, uh, coming attraction. If you'd rather not, then write down something else. The most important thing for *you* to bring to the party is, as always, lots of enthusiasm.

Your sweetheart will sure be enthusiastic when he walks through the door – especially if he has the videotape! After fast-forwarding through the movie, start the real show. Focus your attention on his **penis**. Play with it. Talk to it! Men have very close, personal relationships with their genitals, almost as if they're dear friends. Well, show him you feel the same way. Let him see that you cherish his erection. And then, all at once... slide your lips completely down the shaft, as far as you can go, and slowly pull back up.

That first wet, powerful suck is enough to make strong men fall down. Don't go deep on every stroke, though; spend lots of time flicking your tongue around the corona, and rolling the head around your mouth. Don't be afraid to suck hard! I mean *really* hard; his rod can take a lot, as long as you're careful about your teeth. Every time you take the **big plunge**, he'll turn to jelly; men I've interviewed say there's something overwhelming about a deep, hard slide right to the back of the throat.

The classic Deep Throat position – on your back, head hanging back off the edge of the bed – works well and looks great on film, but has one slight drawback: it's hard on the neck. And that's why I was so excited when I found a device called The **Thera-Band Ball**™. It's a big cushy ball, designed so you can stretch out on it and take pressure off your spine. If anyone in your house has back problems, it's a godsend, and worth every penny of $18.50. But right now you're going to discover its greatest potential: it makes "going deep" easy, sexy and comfortable!

Your lover will be puzzled when he first spots it in your bedroom, but as soon as you arch your back across it – and smile an exceptionally wicked smile – he'll figure it out. You're upside down as you take him in your mouth, but this time, your head and neck are perfectly cradled by the soft rubber ball... and your back is getting a **terrific massage**. Believe me, you can spend a *lot* of time in this position. (And so can he, when it's his turn to ride the ball!) In the meantime, along with the greatest oral sex he's ever known, your mate is getting the visual treat of a lifetime. Breasts thrust in the air, tummy stretched flat – hey, you look fantastic, and fantastically sexy.

At last. A ball game you can *both* enjoy every weekend.

"Soon I felt her mouth.
I had still a sort of semi hard on.
She got it into her mouth
and she began to caress it with
her tongue. I saw stars."

-Henry Miller, Tropic of Capricorn

Take Me Out To The "Ball" Game

There are no rules for this game,

and only one eligibility requirement:

A Louisville Slugger,

suitable for stroking, tugging, squeezing and sucking.

And rubbing, licking, nibbling and coming.

If you have one, bring it along with

____ _____

To: _____

This: _____ *evening*

Game time: _____ *o'clock*

You bring the bat; I've got the ball. And don't be late.

You won't want to miss my first pitch.

52 Invitations to Grrreat Sex

n u m b e r 50

Naked Ambition

For Her Eyes Only

*EROTICISM: The powerful force within us
from which spring desire and creativity and
our deepest knowledge of the universe.*

n u m b e r **5 0**

Naked Ambition

i n g r e d i e n t s

- Music
- Drinks
- Candles
- Belt
- More patience than *he* has!

- A place to tie his wrists (If your headboard won't do, then loop the ribbon around one leg of the bed frame)
Bonus points! Indulge in "B&D Lite" by using a small whip, with a leather cup to protect his privates. (Available at adult boutiques)

He Brings:
Red ribbon
A good attitude... *or else!*

*T*he penis is such an amazing thing.

Before I learned how to enjoy my own sexuality, I used to envy men their easy orgasms. Just a touch and *pow*, it's hard; a few strokes and a squeeze and then *bang*, instant pleasure. How cool!

But there's a downside to having such easy access to **orgasm**. *Most guys never learn to pace themselves.* That thing just takes over their brains and slams the accelerator to the floor: go faster! Faster! Next stop, Jizztown!

This is not good. Well, it's not *bad* since, after all, the end result is still an orgasm. But it's like downing a Godiva in a single bite: it can be so much better if you take your time to savor it. Your sweetheart is going to learn that lesson this week... because *you* are going to take charge of his penis, and give him the kind of sex that will **invade** his dreams.

Your date starts in the living room with hugs and kisses, and perhaps a glass of wine. After lots of fun flirting, ask him to show you his *ribbon* – the long red ribbon you specified in your invitation. Loop it around his neck and pull his face to yours for another kiss. Then get up and, leading him by his "**leash**," take him into your candlelit bedroom. Lay him on the bed, then climb on top; put his wrists together over his head and wrap the ribbon around them. Tie the other end to your headboard.

Now begin your slow torture. Straddle his hips and start a slow, sensuous grind. Once you sense a certain stirring down there... stop. Get off. Go change the music. Come back and open his zipper; tug his pants down just far enough to expose his growing **erection**, give it a few long, friendly squeezes... then stop. Go freshen your glass of wine. Let him watch you wriggle out of your skirt and open your blouse. By now his penis crying out *do me do me do me,* but please... take your time.

Use every trick to light his fuse, but take a break before each building explosion. Draw his shaft into your mouth, as far as you can. Don't assume he's not aroused if he's only semi-rigid at this point; he'll enjoy every exquisite lick, every warm **caress**. Once you've brought him back to full attention... *stop*. Make certain he knows just who is in control.

Press his erection flat against his belly and nibble the underside of his shaft like an ear of corn. Fondle his testicles; tickle his anus (and if you know he likes it, slide a lubricated finger inside.) *Stop*. Grab a leather belt from his closet. Watch his eyes pop when you drag it across his trembling manhood; hear him moan when you lasso that bad boy and **tug on it**. Double the belt lengthwise and put his penis between the two strips of leather. Slowly slide the belt back and forth so the leather caresses two sides of his shaft at once.

Spank his cock. Gently, of course, but unmistakably; tap the end of the belt against his one-eyed friend. If you're feeling truly wicked, make him put on a leather cup, available at adult boutiques – then lightly pop him with a belt or even a small **whip**. He's protected, but oh, what a sight, what spectacular sound effects, what trust.

Each time you bring him to the brink, the pressure builds. His nerves sing a little louder, the potential for pleasure grows greater. Four or five cycles later... push him over the edge....

Stroke, fast and hard, while his testicles contract, his crown flushes and swells, his butt rises off the bed, and keep going until that powerful, overheated organ finally, mercifully, **explodes**. Shock waves radiate from his balls, through the bed, through the floor. Your *neighbors* will feel the earth move after this orgasm. In fact...

... you know those tiny earthquakes that keep making the news in California? Yep. The epicenter is my Jeff!

EROTICISM:
The powerful force within us
from which spring desire and
creativity and our deepest
knowledge of the universe.

You are invited to experience

The Kind Of Sex That Will Invade Your Dreams

The formula is explosive, yet simple:

Take one aroused woman with some brand new tricks

Add one sexy man with a long, hard fuse

Wrap with warm sheets, immerse in hot music

and wait for the sparks to fly

There's one more crucial ingredient, which you must bring with you:

One Red Ribbon

at least six feet long

The dream begins at _____ o'clock

Day: _____

Place: _____

R.S.V.P.

You are going to score, so show me your victory dance.

After your next shower. Without your towel.

52 Invitations to Grrreat Sex

n u m b e r 5 1

Lip Service

FOR HIS EYES ONLY

"A honeymoon is not a place-it's a state of mine."

- Gregory J.P. Godek

n u m b e r **5 I**

Lip Service

i n g r e d i e n t s

- Scarf
- Rich soap and lotion for foot bath
- Cup of hot tea
- Champagne
- Limber lips
- Trained tongue

She Brings:
Peppermints, and other interesting things to suck on

"No kissing!"

Remember that line? Julia Roberts, the world's most unlikely hooker, said it to Richard Gere in *"Pretty Woman."* That No Kissing rule is common among prostitutes, which is kind of surprising, considering what they *will* do. But here's why:

It's too intimate. Kissing is much more special than intercourse; you can't even buy it. Women adore it, and often complain about the lack of lip action from their **sweeties**. As for me, well, I don't think it's possible to get enough kisses!

The best we can hope for is *more*... and that's just what you're going to give your lover this week. More kisses, in more shapes and flavors, delivered in more surprising ways than she's ever had before, starting even before her invitation arrives in the mail:

Sunday   Without warning, pull off the road in a secluded spot. Grab her and lock lips!

Monday   Breakfast: Drop in while she's in the shower, pull her wet lips to yours and *smooch!* Dinner: Tie a scarf over her eyes. Now nibble and suck and kiss every inch of her neck and shoulders.

Tuesday   Breakfast: Ever so gently, suck her top lip. Kiss some more, then switch; softly nibble and suck her bottom lip. Repeat until her knees go weak. Dinner: Take the phone from your mate. Tell the caller to *"hold on, please,"* then deliver a deep, passionate kiss. Wink... hand her the phone... and walk away.

Wednesday   Breakfast: After her shower, shower the back of her knees with hot kisses. Dinner: Chase her, catch her, wrestle her onto the sofa. Pin her down with a long, strong, toe-curling kiss.

Thursday   Breakfast: A quick kiss before leaving, then... turn around and come back for more! Dinner: Quickly turn off all the lights in the house. In the sudden darkness, grab her for a lo-o-o-ooong and juicy kiss.

Friday   Breakfast: Kiss the open palm of her hand, then roll her fingers into a fist. Whisper in her ear, *"Save this in case of emergencies...."* Dinner: Give her a luxurious foot bath. As you dry her feet, gently nibble each toe.

Saturday   Breakfast: *"Honey, it looks like... well, like your face needs a little dusting. Good thing I have the right tool for the job!"* Move your lips all over her face, lightly sucking in as you go. Dinner: Ahh, the **big date** arrives, and things get really interesting....

Greet your lover, naturally, with a kiss. And then a *scratch*. That's right – scratch her lightly along her shoulders, then retrace your route with kisses. Like a backrub, we forget how incredible a good scratch can feel until we get one. Alternating them with kisses is a classic lover's treat, so ancient it's described in the **Kama Sutra**. Run your nails down her back... then kiss where you touched. Scratch her thighs, then kiss them. Switch until you've electrified every inch of her skin.

Take a swallow of hot tea, then drop down to her sweet puss. The heat of your mouth on her clitoris may levitate her bare bottom right off the bed. After a while, ask her for one of the peppermints she brought; pop it in your mouth and deliver a blast of cool refreshment to her lips... then do the same for her *other* lips. Oh, and here's one of my favorites: champagne kisses. A mouthful of bubbly adds sparkle to kisses anywhere you put them! Make her nipples snap, crackle and pop. Douse her *mons* and then slurp up the fizzy stuff. Just as with those **erotic scratches**, alternate between contrasting sensations: follow each chilly splash with the soft warmth of your tongue.

No doubt she'll want to practice her kisses, too, and Mr. Stiffy will be more than happy to stand in for you while your mouth stays busy elsewhere. Lick, suck, nibble, bite, and kiss long into the night. Congratulations – you're on your way to becoming a certified Doctor of Love, with a Ph.D. in Kissology...

... and you just passed your oral exams!

"A honeymoon is not a place-
it's a state of mine."

- Gregory J.P. Godek

You are invited to attend

Dr. Love's
College Of Kissology

Topics to be covered (and demonstrated!) include:

Fast Fun Kisses — Long, Slow Wet Kisses

Wake-Up Kisses — Knock-Out Kisses

Kisses with Teeth — Kisses with Heat

Kisses on Tops — Kisses on Bottoms

And the ever-popular extra credit sections on
Nibbling, Licking, Biting, Sucking, Toes, Necks, Arms, Breasts,
And Lips. (Any Lips!)
Volunteers will be asked to help demonstrate these techniques.

Admission: One Handful of
Peppermint Candies

Date: _____

Time: _____

Classroom: _____

The favor of a reply is requested.

You need only fill your mouth with the

organ of your choice and say,

"Yesh, Ah woo be dewighted to join ooo.

Fank ooo vewy muh."

52 Invitations to Grrreat Sex

number 52

I Put A Spell On You

For Her Eyes Only

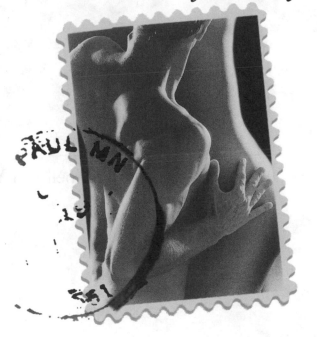

"I don't sleep with married men,
but what I mean is that I don't sleep with
happily married men."

-Britt Ekland, Swedish actress

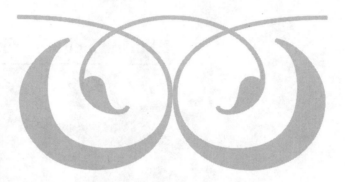

n u m b e r 52

I Put A Spell On You

---

i n g r e d i e n t s

- (I suggest you grab his *wallet* and rub it on your body to cast the spell in your invitation... but don't tell him until he pays for dinner! He'll never open it again without smiling.)
- 1 movie
- 1 dinner

- 1 confident enchantress, with lots of love potion

(Nature's Plus Natural Beauty Cleansing Bar is pH 4.5; call 1-800-937-0500)

He Brings:
1 fine artist's brush
1 magic wand (Cast the right spell and watch it levitate!)

*P*ussy.

That's such a beautiful word. Sure, it's not something you'd say in public, but that doesn't mean it's vulgar – just private, like sex itself. Go ahead, whisper it right now. *Pussy.* That soft breathy pop, sliding into a long, sensuous *essss.....* I just love the word. It's pretty, like the part it describes.

Men adore it, and everything it stands for. They love the way it looks and feels, the happy way it responds to their touch. Oh, and they **go *wild*** when they catch a hint of its wonderful, sexy scent. That's something no chemist has ever duplicated; just a few molecules of it can go ripping straight through any man's brain, lighting up neurons like a Christmas tree. At a deep, fundamental level, that fragrance is the source of every woman's power.

I know that a lot of women don't feel that way about their scent. They're worried that their guy finds it unpleasant. *Put that thought out of your head immediately.* If you're in reasonably good health and freshly bathed, you smell great. (But as long as we're on the topic: did you know that your bath soap may be bad for your pussy? The vagina has a lower pH balance than the rest of your skin, which seems to be nature's way of making that warm, **moist spot** unfriendly to bacteria and yeast. If you have a recurring problem with infections or odor, try a low-pH lactic-acid-balanced soap.)

I know men who will rinse their faces after performing oral sex, but will not use soap, just so they can smell that incredibly erotic fragrance as they go about their business. This week, you're going to treat your lover to that same **delicious** feeling, and put on a show that will electrify him.

Plan your seduction for early afternoon so he'll have the whole evening to enjoy your treat. Tell him you want to take him to a movie, but first... push him on the bed. Roll around, wrestle, tickle and play. Ask him for the *brush*. Your invitation specified a soft, supple artist's brush; once you're both bare, run the smooth bristles over his skin. Twirl it around his nipples; stroke his face with it. He may imagine that this is the whole **seduction** – a flick of sable followed by sex – but he's wrong. Wa-a-aayyy wrong.

Prop him up on some pillows so he has a good view of you. Play with yourself. Touch that wonderful, mysterious place between your legs; your love garden, your little fox, your kitty, your yoni, your **luscious lips**, your honey pot... your *pussy.* Make it wet.

And then dip the brush into it. Moisten the tip with your girl juice, then smile... and paint your sacred scent on his upper lip, like a tiny mustache. His jaw will drop, his thoughts will stutter, and in that instant he will fall under your spell. Moisten the brush again, and dab a bit of liquid sex behind his ears. *"Ohhh, this is just the best perfume I have... and I want you to smell it all day long today...."*

Paint his nails with it! Sweep it under his chin. Soon, of course, you'll throw the brush in the corner; it's time to rock and push and thrust against his raging **erection**. Ride him until you both feel that extraordinary tingle, that tightening in the toes and legs and buttocks that signals the approach of a powerful, bodyquaking climax.

Afterwards, wash his tender parts gently with a steamy wet cloth, but as for the rest of him... well, he's still clean enough from his morning shower. Get dressed, and head out to your matinee. He'll be the only one in the theater smiling through the serious parts! But then, he's got his own private form of entertainment: tiny hints of *you* drifting up into his nose, triggering a cascade of happy hormones and thrilling **memories**. Later, at dinner, his conversation might seem a bit odd; every few minutes he'll pause... and inhale... and grin. But the real magic of your love potion is that it's *addictive*, and it won't be long before he's desperate for another fix.

Check, please!

"*I don't sleep with married men, but what I mean is that I don't sleep with happily married men.*"

-Britt Ekland, Swedish actress

I Put A Spell On You

Like all good magic, it started with something of yours —

something small and personal. You use it all the time.

I slipped it between my breasts, rolled it over a nipple.

I touched it to my lips... and then pressed it between my hips.

And now that you've touched it, my spell is working.

Your pulse quickens. Your smile broadens. Ahhh, yes...

You are beginning to think about Sex!

Bring 1 small, fine, soft and supple Artist's Paintbrush

if you wish to experience the full power of my magic

Date: _____

Time: _____

Location: _____

R.S.V.P.

After I step out of the shower, approach me from behind.

Lean low. Then kiss the back of my knees

until I melt.

Specialty Shops

For adult products, ideas, catalogs, and unusual items, including many of the products mentioned in this book, call the following companies.

Mail-Order Catalogs

Good Vibrations
1210 Valencia Street
San Francisco, Ca 94110
(800)289-8423
www.goodvibes.com

Xandria
165 Valley Drive
Brisbane, CA 94005
(800)242-2823   (415)468-3812

Behind Closed Doors
P.O. Box 93
Woonsocket, RI 02895-0779
(800)350-3314

Adam and Eve
P.O. Box 800
Carrboro, NC 27510
(919)644-1212 (800)274-0333

Blowfish
2261 Market Street #284
San Francisco, CA 94114-284
(415) 252-4340 (800)325-2569

Victoria Secret
(800)888-8200

1-800-FLOWERS - A very unique flower company
• The calender club allows you to pre-register for as many flower dates as you desire... And on those dates, they'll send flowers to your honey automatically.

• With the flora minder program, the 800 flower folks will call or write to remind you of important upcoming dates.

Celebration Fantastic
A catalogue of wit and whimsy, nonsense and necessities. Neat cool, one-of-a-kind romantic gifts! Call now for your free catalogue!

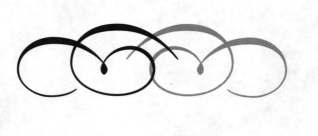